by kids for kids

A Kid's Guide to Giving

Freddi Zeiler

innovative KIDS
Hands-On • Minds-On

Written by Frederika Zeiler. Ms. Zeiler is represented by By Kids For Kids Co.™ By Kids For Kids Co. is a leading organization entirely dedicated to inspiring and motivating the innovative spirit within every kid. By Kids For Kids Co. inspires and rewards kids for innovation excellence and encourages young people to pursue problem solving in their educations and careers. By Kids For Kids Co. represents some of the most brilliant young minds in America. Please go to www.bkfk.com for more information.

Written by Freddi Zeiler
Illustrations by Ward Schumaker
Designed by Ph.D, www.phdla.com
www.innovativekids.com

To my family for their support and love;

to Topanga Canyon for my inspiration;

to Kate Torpie for all of her hard work as the project was developed;

and to Michael Hodgson, for his faith in me.

CONTENTS

A Message from Freddi Zeiler

I always thought my life was normal. I lived in a house with my mom, dad, and two younger sisters. My mom drove me to school every morning in our van. I would learn about fractions or mammals or Benjamin Franklin and then come home and do my homework and have dinner with my family. That didn't seem unusual to me. I did it every day—so did everyone else I knew, and so that was it. Nothing special. And that's what I thought for the first thirteen years of my life.

Then in seventh grade, I started watching the news and reading newspapers. I started to learn about things that were going on in other parts of the world. I learned that there were kids in the world whose families couldn't afford to send them to school; instead, these kids had to work to earn money so their families could buy food. I learned about people who didn't have money for medicine when they were sick, and I learned that the environment was being damaged by pollution. I learned that trees were being cut down from rain forests, and animals were losing their homes.

All of these things made me realize that my life wasn't normal. I was really, really lucky! I went to school, I lived in a clean neighborhood, I could go to the doctor when I was sick, and I never went to bed hungry. There were kids in the world, who were my age, who didn't have any of these things, simply because they were born without them. There were people whose lives weren't happy, healthy, and secure, like mine. It didn't seem fair to me, so I decided to help.

I wanted to donate the money from my piggy bank to a charity. Even though it was only a small amount, it was a start. But where to begin? There were so many charities—and many seemed so alike. How could I truly know if a particular charity was any good? Where exactly would my money go? I got frustrated, because I really wanted my donation to matter. I started to research charities on the computer. I spent days and days researching and learning about many different organizations. I wanted to know how they worked, inside and out, so I started e-mailing them and asking questions like, "What do you do?" and "Where does my money go?" I made a folder with all the basic information on a few different charities that I liked so I could compare them.

I didn't originally intend to write a book. Actually, it was my mom who gave me the idea. She said that since I had so much information, I should just put it all together, so other kids wouldn't have to go through the same trouble I had. That way, I would be encouraging others to give, which is another way of making a difference.

Putting a book together was a very difficult thing (just in case any of you ever decide to do it), and I didn't do it alone, either. My sister Hannah helped me research and call the charities, while my parents taught me about money and answered my questions when I got confused. My neighbor Michael Hodgson, who is one of the partners at the design office, Ph.D, found out that I was writing a book and spent a tremendous amount of time trying to help me put it all together and find someone to publish it. Seven years later, with the help of a wonderful organization called By Kids For Kids, everything finally came together. My book has grown and changed in the process, and now it is not only a guide to giving money but to volunteering, donating goods, and organizing charity events as well.

I am now twenty years old, and I go to college at the University of California, Berkeley. I still give my time and money to those in need, because to me it's more than a responsibility or an obligation. It's something that I enjoy, something I do because I care and want to make a difference. That's why I want to pass this information on to you; you can make a difference, too. You're a lucky person; don't you want to share your good fortune with others?

There are about 75 million people under the age of 18 in America. What if every one of you gave 25 cents to a cause? What if every one of you spent an hour doing volunteer work? Put all that money and time together, and you can change the world! So please: read this book, share it with your friends . . . and, most importantly, find room in your heart to give your money, time, and effort to causes that need help. It's the best way to say thank you to the world that has given you so much!

what is a "charitable cause" and why should I give?

The world is a big place, with lots of wonderful things in it. But it also has many problems. It's human nature to want to fix problems and stop suffering; we always want to make things better. That's one of the greatest things about human beings: we care.

You may wonder how to show you care in a way that makes a difference. "I'm just one person," you might say, or "I'm just a kid. What kind of difference can I really make?" The problems seem so big; you feel so small. Many people who want to help wind up doing nothing, because they don't know where to start.

That's what a charity is for. A charity is a group of

people working together on a "charitable cause", a problem that causes suffering that is too big for any one person to fix on his or her own. By joining together with other people who care, YOU have the power to help. Think about a charitable cause that concerns you. Is there a kind of animal you are worried about? A group of people who need help? A part of the environment that is in danger? By the end of this book, you'll know how to get involved—and be ready to make a difference!

Types of Charitable Causes

Many charitable causes have been around for a long time. For example, people have been trying to help the poor for hundreds of years. You may wonder why you should try to fix a problem that nobody has figured out how to solve for such a long time—isn't it pointless? Definitely not! You can help many, many people who don't have the money to buy food, clothing, or get shelter. And even if you haven't solved the whole problem, helping out even just one person makes a huge difference.

Some huge problems, such as natural disasters, can strike suddenly and require immediate attention. For example, Hurricane Katrina ripped the city of New

Orleans apart in a matter of days. Volunteers and donations were needed, and fast. Many people rushed to help out, raising millions of dollars in just a few weeks. People offered to share their homes with people who had nowhere to live. The sudden need for charity brought out the best in people, and the assistance and donations that people gave helped make the situation more bearable for thousands of people.

Many charitable causes already have established organizations dedicated to them. These organizations, like the Red Cross, Greenpeace, and the American Humane Association, already have a system for getting help where it is needed. But that doesn't mean they don't need your help. In fact, you're the reason these organizations can exist! If people like you didn't offer their help, these organizations would have nothing to work with.

As you try to decide what causes matter most to you, you may come up with some that are not represented by any organization. The issue may be so new (an animal that only recently became endangered, or a disease that was just discovered) that no organizations exist yet to help. Or the cause may be so small (a park in your neighborhood that needs to be cleaned up or a family in your town that lost its home to a fire) that no one has thought to organize people to help. If that's the case, then it's up to you! It can be challenging to do it on your own, without some big organization behind you, but it can also be more fulfilling. You'll learn about lots of things you can do to help a cause like this as you read this book. Don't be discouraged. Nothing can stop you from helping if you want to badly enough.

Why Should You Help?

The first reason you should help is simple: the world needs you! As wonderful as our planet is, it has lots of problems, big and small. To solve these problems and make the world a better place for everyone to live, all of us—including YOU—need to cooperate, to work together as a community. Even though you might think you're "just a kid," you are a full-fledged member of the global community. You share the planet with people around the globe, with animals that live on the land and in the seas, with forests and rivers and mountains. As part of this gigantic family, we all have a responsibility to care for one another.

Right now, children your age are starving in African countries. Does it bother you to know that as you read this, they are exhausted from hunger and their empty stomachs are grumbling? Sure it does, and it should—these hungry people are no different from you. They were just born into a less fortunate local community. But they're still part of your global community. By giving, you CAN make the world a better place for them.

Right now, thousands of acres of Amazon rain forest are being cut down each day. Does it bother you to know that millions of ancient trees are dying and countless animals will have nowhere to find food or shelter? Sure it does. You may not think you have a lot in common with rain forest plants and animals, but you do. You share the world with them; they are part of the global community, too. Rain forests help human beings by purifying the air we breathe and by providing potential cures for countless human diseases. Don't they deserve our help in return? Forests, plants, and animals don't have the power to help themselves, but does that mean they deserve to be destroyed? Who will take care of these parts of Earth, if not EACH one of us?

Another reason to give is because you want to give back. Think about all the great things you are lucky enough to have in this world. Do you have love and joy in your life? A family, a home, food on the table? Take a minute to be grateful for these simple things. Not everyone is so lucky. These things are gifts, and you can pass them on. Giving back to the world is the best way to show how much you appreciate the good things in your life.

Another big reason to give is that it gives you more faith in yourself. When you save money every week to give to a struggling local animal shelter, you'll discover that you have more generosity, determination, and willpower than you ever gave yourself credit for. When you spend time caring for abused animals in a local shelter, you'll discover that you have deep wells of compassion and gentleness. Those are important qualities for a person to have! Nurturing them in yourself is worth your time and effort.

The last big reason to give back to the world is to give yourself hope for the future. Being part of the giving community reminds you that all problems are solvable. When you gather food to contribute to a food bank, you'll realize that all it takes is more people like you to solve the problem of hunger in your community. When your family and friends follow your lead and contribute to a cause, you'll see that others really do care and are willing to help. When you work with an international organization to solve a problem, you'll see that there are hundreds of thousands of people like you all over the world, who are willing to work for change. These are the things that will make the future of our world bright!

All around our globe, every second of every day, people are working to make the world a better place. Who are these amazing people out there changing the world? They are people just like you!

How Much Should You Give?

So you've decided that you want to make a difference. But how much time or money should you give? You may feel like you're supposed to give every penny you've got and spend every spare minute volunteering. But that's really not necessary. Giving back doesn't mean giving away everything.

Think about your money for a moment. You probably don't think you have a whole lot. What you do have, you need to spend to have fun with your friends, to buy presents for people, and to save up for buying things you really want. Not much to spare, you think. But suppose you put a quarter away every day. You'd barely notice it. But by the end of the year, you'd have almost $100! A charity could do a lot with that money!

Now apply that logic to giving time. You are already busy with school, sports, maybe a part-time job. You help out at home, and you need to have fun with your friends, too. These are important parts of your life. But what if you turned off the TV for just one hour once a week? You could use that hour to really make a difference—walking dogs at a shelter, visiting with an older person at a nursing home, or cleaning up litter in the park. Now imagine doing this every week for a year. What a difference you could make!

It's easy to feel overwhelmed when you first start thinking about giving your time and money to a charitable cause. But getting involved with charity works the same way school projects do—step by step. Once you start to help, even the largest problems seem smaller. Only people who act can change the world—and it's easy for you to become one of them. You don't have to give all your time and money to make a difference to a charitable cause. You just have to *give!*

One Dime at a Time

Did you ever wonder why President Franklin Delano Roosevelt's face is on the dime? In 1938, President Roosevelt founded The National Foundation for Infantile Paralysis. Its goal was to defeat polio, a disease which had killed or paralyzed thousands of Americans in the early twentieth century. President Roosevelt himself had lost the use of his legs to polio.

The organization asked every person in the United States to give just a dime to fight the disease. They knew that tiny donations from a huge amount of people would add up to a lot of money! One famous radio celebrity, Eddie Cantor, nicknamed this campaign "The March of Dimes."

Men, women, and children alike sent their dimes to the cause. With every ten-cent donation, they got closer to fig-uring out a polio vaccine. Finally in 1955, the vaccine was ready! It had been discovered by a scientist named Dr. Jonas Salk, whose research had been funded by the March of Dimes. Today, all children in America can get a vaccina-tion that will protect them from this dreaded disease.

NOTES

how do I choose a charitable cause to contribute to?

You understand why charity is important, and you've decided to take the plunge and do something about it. You're ready to make a difference! Now . . . how do you turn the overwhelming idea of starting into the manageable act of starting? Step by step.

Step 1: Look Into Your Heart

The best way to decide on a charitable cause to help is to look into your heart. Think about a story you've heard that caused you to put the paper down and say, "I can't read anymore." Maybe you've seen a news report that made you gasp or cover your eyes. In fact, many people turn their heads when they see real suffering, because they find it too painful to watch. But that doesn't help anyone. It isn't right to ignore suffering when you can do something about it. And you CAN do something about it. It takes strength to look suffering in the eye and vow to change it. And each time you fulfill that vow, you help to end suffering and you get more strength. When a cause affects you so much that you don't think you can stand to know about it, chances are, you're the perfect person to help. It's painful, because you care.

Sometimes, it takes an event in our own lives to show us how the world can use our help. Maybe you found your dog on the street and have now become involved in helping other strays. Perhaps you watched a grandparent who bravely fought an incurable disease, and now you want to help find a cure. If you are having trouble deciding on which cause is closest to your heart, look to your own life experience. Life can inspire you to get involved. It can take you down the path that's right for you!

There are all sorts of charitable causes. You just have to decide what issues are closest to your heart.

Environmental causes: What is your environment? On a small scale, your environment is your neighborhood and your town. Maybe you are concerned about littering in a local park or a new building that will destroy a local forest. But that's not your whole environment—remember, you are a citizen of the world. Earth is your environment. There are many national and even international environmental causes that need your charity. Oceans and rivers are being polluted, chemicals have made a hole in the atmosphere, and global warming may be melting the polar ice caps. Organizations like the Sierra Club, Friends of the Earth, and Greenpeace all help to make the world a cleaner, safer place for us—and the animals and plants with whom we share our environment. And charity is desperately needed for environmental causes. The Earth needs caretakers—and you can be one.

Animal causes: Maybe your heart breaks when you hear about animals in need. Tigers are being hunted to extinction, wolves are losing their habitat, and even worse, many cosmetic companies perform cruel and unnecessary tests on animals. Defenders of Wildlife and the World Wildlife Fund both help animals around the world. Locally, your shelter

Wild Animals as Pets

The exotic animal trade is an international money-maker. Thanks to the Internet, business is booming. Poachers trap wild and often endangered animals in one country and sell them in another. Many animals are shipped illegally to buyers around the world. It is not unusual for an animal to become ill or die along the way. These animals desperately need your help!

In the United States, tiger cubs are a popular pet. What happens when these large carnivores grow up? Many people find they can't take care of them—after all, they are wild animals. Organizations like Big Cat Rescue in Tampa, Florida, take in abused, neglected, and unwanted big cats. It's amazing that here in the United States, there are unwanted tigers. Meanwhile, in the wild, these great animals are close to going extinct.

could probably use a helping hand. Dogs and cats living in cages could use all the kindness you can spare. What's great about local shelters is that you get to do a lot of hands-on work. While international organizations accept donations, a local shelter may need your help walking dogs or socializing newborn kittens.

Human causes: As people, we are drawn to help other people—it's just so easy to imagine yourself in someone else's shoes when you see them in need of help. How often have you given away half of your lunch to a friend who forgot his or hers? No one wants to see other people suffer. Yet, around the world, people are suffering right now—and they need a lot more than half of a sandwich. Some families are homeless, while others are literally starving to death. Some children your own age have spent their entire lives in war-torn countries. You know that no one deserves to live in fear—to never know the peace of a good night's sleep. Organizations like Save the Children bring food to kids who do not have enough because of war or poverty. They also bring hope and a little joy to children who have so little.

People who are ill also need charity and kindness. Despite modern medicine, there are many deadly and crippling diseases in the world today. Charitable organizations like the Cystic Fibrosis Foundation raise money to try to find cures for these diseases. This kind of organization needs people like you to help by donating money or volunteering.

But it's not only about finding cures. A neighbor with a sick family member may need charity, too. Long-term illnesses can be so expensive that many families cannot afford medical treatment. Imagine if money was the only thing keeping a member of YOUR family from recovering! You could help by raising money.

Another way to help ill people is to spend time with

Watch Your Step

Many countries set up landmines during wartime. Landmines work like underground bombs: if you step on one, the mine explodes, causing injury or death. Sadly, thousands of landmines are still active—even in countries that are no longer at war. In some rural areas, walking to the store can be dangerous. In Cambodia, more than 700 innocent people were hurt or killed because of landmines in 2003. Around the world, 15,000–20,000 people are killed or hurt each year as a result of explosives left over from wars that have ended.

Charitable organizations like the International Campaign to Ban Landmines are working to stop all that. The International Mine Ban Treaty makes the use, production, selling, and stockpiling of mines illegal. It also requires that governments clean old minefields and offer assistance to victims. As of 2006, 149 countries had signed this document. That's a HUGE step, and it will save thousands of innocent lives each year.

them. When people don't feel well, they could really use comfort and companionship. Sick or elderly people in nursing homes are often lonely. Your once-a-week visit could be the treat that someone looks forward to all week.

Human rights is another important charitable cause. Human rights deals with people who suffer from illnesses, poverty, starvation, or pain—because of unfair laws. In some places, children are forced to work in dangerous factories for long hours. Women do not have the same rights as men. Global organizations like Amnesty International fight for human rights around the world. They protect women, children, and others in need. Which is not to say that the fight for rights is not happening in our own backyard. For example, the Equal Rights Amendment, which gives women the same rights as men, was written in 1923. Seems like common sense, right? And yet . . . as of right now, it STILL hasn't been added to our Constitution. Throughout our history, citizens—especially minorities—have had to fight for equal rights in this country. Many are still fighting. Sure, there are laws in place to protect our rights, but these laws are not always upheld.

In the end, which charitable cause you choose is less important than the fact that you have decided to get involved. As with any new experience, it's probably best to take your best guess and dive in. What you learn will help you focus your interests in the future, and you are bound to make a positive difference no matter which organizations you choose to help.

Step 2: Get the Facts!

So you want to help. You've picked a cause. You're ready to jump in. You certainly CAN jump right in. There's nothing stopping you! But you may want to learn more about your cause before you give. Maybe you already knew that the environment needed help. But did you know that pollution in the ocean leads to less oxygen for people to breathe? It's true. Maybe you also know that illiteracy is a problem—but would you be surprised to hear that about 16% of the world's adult population cannot read? Would you be more motivated to help if you knew exactly how many people in your own town couldn't read? Find out the facts.

It won't be easy. What you will learn might make you angry or sad. The truth about suffering can be hard to

A Civil Rights Victory

In the 1950s, it was normal for schools in the United States to be racially segregated. Only white students could go to white schools, and black students could only go to black schools.

An African-American third-grader named Linda Brown had to walk a mile to her school in Topeka, Kansas, crossing several tracks in a train yard on the way. However, there was a "whites-only" school just seven blocks from her home. Her father, Oliver Brown, was so angry that he fought for his daughter's right to attend that school. He fought all the way to the Supreme Court.

How did he do it? A non-profit organization called the National Association for the Advancement of Colored People Legal Defense and Education Fund, which had teams of well-trained lawyers, volunteered to take on the case. (They were led by a lawyer named Thurgood Marshall, who later became the first African-American Supreme Court justice.)

Other non-profit groups, including the American Civil Liberties Union, wrote opinions that the Supreme Court took into consideration during the case. In 1954, these volunteer groups finally won their case—and that's why segregated schools are illegal in our country today.

hear. Yet, the truth can also inspire you to help—and show you that you have strengths you never knew about. That alone is a great reason to learn as much as you can.

But there are other reasons. For example, the more you know, the more you can share. Soon, YOU'LL be the one educating others. Spreading the word IS a form of charity—you could inspire others to help, too. Learning more about a cause also helps you figure out what kind of help is needed. You may find that the problem is worst in one specific part of the world; maybe you'll decide to focus your help there. The more you know, the easier it will be to find a good place to start.

So where do you learn about your cause? You can read about charitable causes in newspapers, magazines, and books. You can look online or talk to experts in the field. Teachers, librarians, and parents can often help you find more information.

Step 3: Find an Organization

Locating a charity is easy. All you have to do is look in the back of this book for a great list of reputable charities. You can also look online—most large charitable organizations have web sites. There are even web sites designed

Trustworthy Organization Expenditures

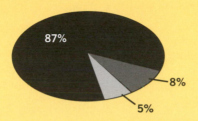

■ Programs ■ Fund-raising ▫ Management & General

This pie chart shows how a charitable organization might spend donations. Suppose you donated $100. Out of that, $87 would go towards their charitable programs. Another $8 would go towards fund-raising. That means that money is spent trying to get others to donate. So your $8 would go towards publicity, advertising, and fund-raising events. Only $5 of your $100 would go towards paying the salaries of employees and covering the general expenses of running the organization. That's a really good breakdown.

to help you learn about lots of different charities. For example, www.charitynavigator.org provides detailed information about worthy charitable organizations. Type www.youthnoise.com to tap into a variety of causes relevant to young people like yourself. Youth Noise is a web-based platform where youth connect, inspire, and act with one another to build a better world. You can also connect with local charities through web sites like www.volunteermatch.org and www.servenet.org. Take the time to explore different charities. You need to find an organization that specializes in your cause.

Once you find an organization that looks interesting, you should do a little more research. First, find out what their needs are. Are they looking for donations or volunteers? If they are looking for volunteers, are you old enough? If they are accepting donations, find out what percent of the money you donate actually goes to the cause. Most charitable organizations depend on donations to keep running. Some of the money you give will go towards paying the charity's employees, renting their offices, having a web site, and other costs. But almost all of the money people donate should go to helping the cause. Find out what fraction or percentage of the money is spent on the "extras" before you decide to contribute.

Charities Chart

The chart below can help you keep track of your findings. Once you begin giving to a charity, the chart can help you keep track of your activities, too.

Cause	
Organization	
Type of Help They Accept	
Percent of Money That Goes to Cause	
Did I Pick That Organization?	
Kind of Help I Gave	
Date I Gave Help	

Once you have researched several organizations that help your cause, you must decide which to support. For example, maybe you care about a specific endangered bird species. You can give to an organization that helps endangered species in general, such as the World Wildlife Fund. However, you may find an organization that more closely matches your goals. The National Audubon Society is a charity that focuses on birds. Perhaps you want to contribute to it. Or maybe your bird lives in just one place: a forest that is soon to be chopped down. Is there a charity group that is working to protect that forest? Supporting it might be the best way to help your bird.

As you can see, it's not always easy to decide which group to support. Many people would just think, "Well, one group is just as good as another." They might give to whichever group they come across first. Don't do that! Your help is too valuable to give to "just anybody." If you have decided to give away your time or money, don't you want to make sure that your gift makes the biggest difference it can? That's why you should learn as much as you can about the organizations you're thinking about. Read the mission statements on their web sites. A mission statement explains the ultimate goals of the charity. You can also do research on their web sites to find out how much of your donation goes toward the cause you really care

Watch Out

Sadly, there is another reason to research an organization. Some are scams. As awful as it is, there are some con artists who set up fake charities to steal money and personal information. These fakes are hard to resist, because they prey on people's natural instinct to help. That's why many scams begin in response to a sudden disaster.

If you get an e-mail from an organization you haven't heard of, don't give money until you check it out. Don't just visit their web site. Scam web sites can make bogus charities look like real charities. To check, visit the web site for the Better Business Bureau Wise Giving Alliance: www.give.org.

Also you should never give money over the phone. Ask the caller to send information in writing. If the organization is for real, they will be glad to mail you information. Don't give out personal information over the phone, either.

Scams sometimes use a name that is similar to the name of a real organization to try to fool people. Don't be tricked! Your best and safest bet is to approach the charity that YOU choose—not to let a charity choose you.

about, in what parts of the world they have programs, and how their programs work. These factors can help in your decision.

What about those of you who can't find any organizations to help your cause? Maybe you're the person to start one! You can take matters in your own hands and inspire others to help, too. It may sound impossible now—but it's not. You'll be amazed at how willing people are to help and to give. Sometimes, they just need someone to show them how. Your courage and effort WILL inspire others.

Whatever option you choose, don't give up! If your first experience is not what you hoped it would be, then you and your organization are not a good match. Keep trying! Maybe you're lucky: you care about a few different causes. That's okay, too! As you grow older, your interests will change. You may find you want to get involved with different charities or cease giving to some you've been with for a while. It's all up to you. You will KNOW when you find the charity that is RIGHT for you.

how do I contribute?
(Part 1)
By giving money!

So you've chosen a charity, and you know all about the cause and the organization. You may have decided that the best way for you to help is by giving money. Now comes the hard part . . . GETTING the money. There are tons of ways kids can get money to give. You can give your own money. Or you can raise money specifically for your cause. This section is filled with nitty-gritty details about how to get and give money. Don't get bogged down. Just use the details that apply to the way YOU want to give money.

Giving Your Own Money

If you're lucky enough to get an allowance, you can donate

part of that. You shouldn't feel like you ought to donate all of your allowance—it's yours! Keeping some of it for your own use doesn't make you selfish nor does it mean that you are an uncaring person. Only donate as much as you can while STILL being happy with what is left.

Still, it kind of hurts to give over your money, especially if your allowance isn't much to begin with. Perhaps it's hard for you to hold on to money and not spend it. How can you make it hurt less to give your money? How can you make sure you don't spend money you really want to give to charity? Here are a few ideas:

Put it in a jar. Label the jar with something that will inspire you NOT to take the money out for, say, a nice jacket or a new pair of sneakers. These are hard temptations to resist—but you can save for them separately. On your label, you may list the top three reasons you want to give to your cause. And, of course, you will want to write the name of the organization on the label. Draw pictures if it helps. Whenever you have money you want to give to your cause—spare change, gift money, even a quarter you find in the sofa!—put it into the jar and make a tally mark on your label that tells you how much you added. At the end of the year, it will be very satisfying to see how much you've collected for your charity.

Pretend you don't have it. As soon as your parents give you your allowance, take a certain amount of it (perhaps one or two dollars) and put it right into the jar. (Ask your parents to pay you in one-dollar bills to make this easier.) If you find it hard to give up the money for the jar, you could ask your parents to hold on to a certain amount every time. (Somehow it's easier to give away money that you've never actually laid your hands on!) Decide on a target number—$25 or $50 perhaps—and keep track of how much they're holding for you. When you reach your target, collect the money from your parents, and make your donation!

Give up something small. Say you buy sodas from the machine at school a couple of times a week. Can you live without them? Sure you can! Each time you skip that soda, put the money you would have spent on it some-where special—maybe in that jar or in an envelope marked with the name of your charity. You'll hardly miss those sodas . . . and the money will pile up more quickly than you think.

Spare some change! Every time you buy something, use whole dollar bills, not exact change; that way, you'll get change back from the cashier. Put that change in your pocket. Every day before bed, empty your pocket right into your charity jar!

No matter where your money comes from, setting aside part of it for charity can be hard. There are temptations every-where. But if you can do it, it will give you a great sense of strength and purpose.

Cash Gifts

Maybe you don't get an allowance. You're not alone— lots of kids don't. But you might still get money from friends or relatives as a gift on a special occasion. The next time that happens, why not give back? Donate part of that gift to your favorite charity.

"Hey," you may think, "but the money was a gift— for me." And that's true. You shouldn't give all of it away. It's okay to enjoy your gift. But you can also make it a policy to donate part of each gift you receive—for example, you can decide that the first $5 of a gift goes into your charity jar or that you always put one-third of the money away for giving.

When you write a thank-you note for your gift, you can even let the gift giver know that you donated part of the money to a charitable cause. You can tell that person all about your cause—and maybe inspire him or her to get involved, too. And who knows—your good deed may inspire your gift giver to give MORE to you next time.

Money You Earn

Maybe you don't get an allowance. Maybe you usually get stuff, not money, for gifts. What can you do to get your hands on some cash? You're going to have to

"I gave $16 of my own money to UNICEF for the tsunami relief. I wanted to spend my money this way, because I knew there were kids just like me who needed a lot of help in this situation." –Lucy, age 9

earn it! What about getting a part-time job?

It can be difficult for students to find jobs. Most stores, restaurants, and other businesses have minimum age requirements, and they often want experience. But that shouldn't stop you from trying. Maybe your neighbors are looking to hire someone to do work for them. Why not you? Having a job is a great way to earn money, meet new friends, and learn new skills.

You can start by asking people you know. It's safe for you, and your potential customers already know and trust you. Just tell them what kind of work you're looking for. You can put signs up at school, hand out flyers to neighbors, and ask people you know to spread the word. Talk with your parents before advertising yourself or taking on any jobs. Suggest that they find out what, if any, income taxes you may owe on your earnings.

It's great that you want to get a job to earn money for charity. It means you're willing to work for something you care about—which is an amazing personal quality. Don't be shy about telling people that part of your pay will be donated to your favorite charity. It will make them feel even better about hiring you. Remember—people like to give. You may even inspire them to give you a little extra specifically for your charity.

No matter how much you earn at your job, remember that YOU earned that money. You're allowed to have some fun with it! You don't have to give away every last penny in order to be a good, generous person. Only donate what you are comfortable living without—whether you decide to give 10%, 20%, or 50% is up to you. Remember, you should give because you want to.

Deciding How to Use Your Money

Your money is your money. You either worked really hard for it, or it was given to you by someone who wanted you to have it. Either way, you deserve to enjoy it. Don't feel bad about keeping some for fun. It's always good to have some money saved up, too, whether it's stashed somewhere safe in your room or deposited in a bank. So how much of your money can you donate to a cause (or causes) you care a lot about? How do you balance all of these different things that are calling out for your money?

Do what adults do to manage money for their families and businesses: Sit down and make a budget. Start by

Job Ideas

The best kind of job to look for is one that you can get based on skills you've already got. Here are some ideas.

Your Skill	Job Idea
Playing with children	Baby-sitting
Fixing computers	Computer consultant for neighbors
Caring for animals	Pet-sitting; dog walking
Caring for plants	Gardener's helper; plant-sitting
Doing math problems	Math tutor
Taking pictures	Photographer at friends' parties
Playing sports	Private sports lessons; referee
Cooking and serving	Catering assistant
Heavy lifting	Snow shoveling; leaf bagging; spring cleaning

figuring out how much you have—and how much you expect you'll be getting. Then you'll have an idea of how much you have to work with.

Quick Tips for Budgets

Working out a budget is a pretty difficult task. Keeping track of where your money "goes" is hard for kids and adults. That's why it's helpful to keep track of your money with a chart. Your budget should have three headings: Savings, Charity, and Spending. Even before you get money, you can decide to give the same amount or the same percentage each time.

Let's look at this example of a budgeting chart, below. Suppose Ann gets paid every two weeks. In the first check, she makes $300. The total she puts in savings and gives to charity is $150. That leaves $150 for spending. Two weeks later, she only makes $150. She can't give or save as much—or she'd have nothing left for spending. Instead, Ann gives and saves the same percentage—half of what she earned. That leaves her with $75 for spending.

Amount	Date	Savings (20%)	Charity (30%)	Spending (50%)
$300	12/6/05	$60	$90	$150
$150	12/20/05	$30	$45	$75

Safety First!

Donating money to charity is important—but your safety is MORE important. Use your street smarts when it comes to earning money, and keep your parents involved in your decision making; they've got street smarts, too. Here are some general guidelines.

- As a student, you shouldn't take a job that requires late hours. Discuss some reasonable ground rules with your parents, and let your employers know your rules in advance. If you feel uncomfortable with someone who offers you a job, trust your gut. Don't take it—there are other jobs out there!

- If you get a phone call from someone asking to hire you, always ask who gave the caller your name. Then, check with his or her reference before you agree to do the work. If you can't check the reference, say no. If someone asks you to do something that you're not comfortable with, such as pet-sitting a large dog, you don't have to do it.

Most of us have been taught our whole lives to be polite and respectful. But when it's a matter of your safety, you should never worry about hurting someone's feelings. A good person who means you no harm will understand and respect your decision.

Keeping a budget lets you make a plan and stick to it. It allows you to make changes based on your options. You may find, after a few weeks, that you aren't leaving yourself enough fun money—or that you often have money left over. You can keep track of how you spend your money. Each time you make a purchase, write it down. This will help you create a future budget tailored for your lifestyle. When you make your budget, you decide how much you want to put in each section, depending on what's important to you and what you need.

Caring about a charitable cause should never make you feel guilty about having money or having fun. If you give too much of your money away, it can sour your experience with charity. Giving should not make you enjoy your life any less. In fact, it should add joy to your life. So make sure you budget some money for your own enjoyment.

Raising Money

Many people prefer not to take money out of their personal budgets for giving. They've got another strategy for contributing: raising money for their favorite causes.

What's the difference between earning money and raising money? When you earn money, it's yours; you just choose to give some of it to a cause. When you raise money, you're getting cash specifically for a cause—it's never really "yours." All of it goes to your charity. We'll talk about two ways to raise money: sponsored events and fund-raisers. If you take part in a sponsored event, you need to find "sponsors" who give you a donation based on your performance. If you are having a fund-raiser, you collect a set amount of money from donors. Let's compare a few different methods of raising money.

Write a letter. One way to ask for money is the old-fashioned way: letters. Letters have many advantages—they allow a person to think over their decision in private. They don't put the potential donor under pressure. A letter is a physical reminder of your request—each time they see the letter, they are reminded that they still need to give.

A letter is the least invasive method of asking for money. It allows you to explain your cause and why it's important to you—without lecturing your potential sponsor or donor. A letter also gives you a chance to tell someone how much their gift means. It lets them feel like they're part of the action. Also, it shows them that you're serious about this. You've already put in the time and effort to write a good letter.

However, there are a few downsides to letters—they can be thrown away or overlooked. While you can put them in the mailboxes of your neighbors, postage costs could limit how many letters you can send. Another cost: you're more likely to get a donation if you send the donor a pre-stamped envelope to mail back to you. To cut costs, you could send an e-mail. However, e-mails are even more frequently overlooked.

Go door-to-door. The main concern with this method of collecting money is SAFETY. You should never go door-to-door without a parent or guardian—even in your own neighborhood. However, this method does force people to make a decision on the spot—and they may be encouraged to give you a donation right then or allow you to put their name on a list of sponsors. You can also go to stores and businesses and ask them for money. Still, people may feel like you're intruding and not give a donation because of that.

Make phone calls. First of all, only call people you know. You may even ask a parent to approve your list. There may be reasons you shouldn't ask a certain family friend for money— reasons you may not know. Phone calls are the least effective way of getting donations. People may forget to mail out a check that they promised. However, if you are looking for sponsors, this method isn't so bad. All the sponsor needs to do is give their name, address, and promise a certain amount. The actual donation comes after a sponsored event, which you'll learn more about.

Host your own event. It's true—you can hold your own event to raise money for a cause! And in this section, we'll talk more about how to host a sponsored event or a fund-raising event. When you hold an event, all the participants also raise money—for your cause! And, fund-raising events are usually a lot of fun.

Collecting Donations

As we have just discussed, there are lots of ways you can ask people to give you money for your cause. You don't need an event or a holiday—you can just ask. Before you do so, contact your organization and find out if they have any rules you should follow. They may also provide you with tips and answers to questions that donors may ask.

Put a list together of friends, family, and local businesses. Run your list by a parent or guardian. Then, go about collecting funds! Make sure you tell your donors when you plan on sending the money to the organization. Also, make sure you tell them to whom they should write a check—the name of your organization.

Sponsored Events

Many charitable organizations will hold sponsored events

"When the terrorists attacked on September 11th, I got all my friends together. We held a lemonade stand and raised over $400 for the Red Cross. Then, we called a local business and they matched our donation!"–Alyssa, age 12

that you can take part in. How do they work? You and a lot of other interested people make a promise to perform an activity—like running a race or walking a special route. You also agree to find sponsors—people who will pay a certain amount of money based on how you do in that activity.

For example, WalkAmerica is a yearly sponsored event that raises money for the March of Dimes. To participate in WalkAmerica, you find sponsors and ask them to support you. How do they support you? By pledging to give a certain amount of money for each mile you walk. Suppose a neighbor pledges $1 per mile, and you walk 10 miles. That's $10 for your cause. Now, suppose you get 25 sponsors—and they all agree to that amount. You'd raise $250, and none of it is from your own pocket! You can raise a lot of money for your cause through your sponsors. Nobody has to give a lot—but a lot of little contributions add up to one really big donation.

You can find sponsors by using one of the methods mentioned above—letters, visits, e-mails, or phone calls. Once you have your sponsors, you are ready for the big day! Many sponsored events are huge—local restaurants donate food, beverage companies donate energy drinks, crowds line up to cheer people on. There's even music to pump up the participants. Charitable events can be a lot of fun. Plus, you already have two things in common with the people you'll meet: you enjoy the same activity, and you support the same cause. Get a friend to join with you—or a bunch of friends, your family, or your whole soccer team—and there's no limit to what a great time you can have.

These types of events may even teach you something about yourself. When you're competing for charity, your competitive instinct really kicks in. At some point, you realize that the better you do, the more money your sponsors will give your cause! It's all up to you. Just by running a race, you are changing the world. And all those people cheering? They're cheering for you. And you deserve it—you're doing your part to make the world more wonderful.

Sounds like fun, right? So how do you get started? Here's what you do.

Find a sponsored event for a cause you believe in.

Organizations hold walk-a-thons or races that help raise money for all kinds of causes. (For example, the Susan G. Komen Breast Cancer Foundation holds an annual Race for the Cure.) These events are held in various locations throughout the year. Your newspaper may mention local events. You may even see a commercial on TV for an event. However you find out about it, make sure you learn the event details like time and place. There may be age restrictions, so it's a good idea to find out about all the rules, too. Most large events have web sites that you can check for event information. You can also call the organization to inquire.

Find sponsors. Getting sponsors is easier than it may seem. You may feel like you're being rude or annoying asking for money. You're NOT. Here's a fact: People don't often give money without being asked. Yet, charity is a natural impulse. People want to be good. By asking for donations, you give people an opportunity to be charitable. You give sponsors a chance to feel good about themselves. In a way, you help them. And you raise money for your cause! So who can sponsor you? Ask everyone you know. You can even ask your parents if you can use their address books. Family, friends, and neighbors can be solicited. Doctors, dentists, and hairdressers deserve an invite to help, too. Ask parents to bring a sign-up sheet to work. Even local businesses may wish to get involved.

Don't be shy about letting your sponsor know what their gift means to you. Whether you choose to write a letter, call, or drop by, tell potential sponsors about your cause and why it's important to you. Let potential sponsors know where their money will go. Don't be afraid to make the event sound like fun—they may even join you. Most important, be polite. Suggest an amount, such as $1 per lap, for a donation. Then, include a sentence to let sponsors know that any amount—larger or smaller—is more than appreciated. After the event, your organization will usually let the sponsor know how much they owe. They may even send your sponsor a thank-you note—but that doesn't get YOU off the hook. You should send out your own thank-you cards, letting the sponsors know how you did in your event.

Events held by organizations are usually well run;

"I walked to raise money for breast cancer research. It made me feel great. I raised about $1,000." –Emily, age 13

they want it to be easy and fun for you to do your share. If people have a good time at their events, they'll be able to raise more money for a good cause . . . and people will be happy to sign up for another event next time!

Hosting a Fund-raiser

Hosting a fund-raiser can be more fun than just asking for money. And, you can get more donations. With fund-raisers, you perform a service (like washing cars) or supply a product (like cakes and cookies), and your customers pay you money that you then donate to your charity. Since customers know you are raising money for a good cause, they are often more willing to buy your service or product—or they're willing to pay more than they usually would for the same thing.

Of course, hosting any kind of fund-raiser requires a staff. If you're hosting a bake sale, you'll need people to make the baked goods and to help sell them. If it's a car wash, you'll need a group of people who don't mind getting wet and soapy! Ask your friends and family. Chances are, they'll be happy to volunteer. Fund-raisers are fun! If you still need more people to lend a hand, put up flyers asking for volun-

Fund-raising Ideas!

A car wash

Pick a location that is safe but where plenty of drivers will see you . . . and where you'll have access to a hose. Bring soap, sponges, and plenty of dry towels!

A bake sale

Find a spot where a lot of hungry people go, and ask if you can set up a big table to sell baked goods. Ask everyone you know to make something yummy to contribute, and try not to eat the profits!

A potluck dinner

Have everyone bring a dish to share, and charge a fee for admission. A local restaurant might donate their space, or you could make it an outdoor picnic if the weather is nice.

A prize raffle

Ask local businesses to donate prizes for a raffle. Then sell as many numbered raffle tickets as you can, for $1 or $2. Pick one ticket number at random for each prize. Whoever bought that ticket wins that prize!

An auction

Ask friends, neighbors, and local businesses if they will con- tribute items or services that you can auction off. Hold the event in a big room, and offer each item one by one. Whoever is willing to pay the most for each item gets it!

Fund-raising Do's and Don'ts

DO ask friends, family members, and other people you know for funds.

DO NOT go door-to-door asking for money without an adult.

DO send out fund-raising letters and e-mails.

DO NOT ask strangers for donations.

DO ask an adult to hold donations in a safe, secure place.

DO NOT carry cash donations with you.

DO have an adult with you when you ask local businesses and shops for money.

DO NOT ask customers in local businesses for donations.

DO have an adult with you when you ask for donations or pledges at safe, public events like a school basketball game.

DO NOT ask for money in public places without an adult present.

DO let the donor bring the donation to you.

DO NOT go somewhere with a stranger to get a donation.

teers in school or around town. Make sure the flyers say the event will support your charity.

Once you have your staff, pick a time for your event. You'll need to pick a time when the weather is right (if your activity is outdoors), and schedule a rain date, too. Be sure you pick a time far enough in the future that you have time to do everything you need to make your event a success.

You'll also have to pick a place for your event. The type of place you'll need depends on the type of event you're planning. But in general, you need somewhere that people will be able to get to easily and where there are a lot of passersby.

Once you've made all these decisions, you'll need to advertise the event to the general public. The more people who know about your event, the better! Start with flyers. You can pass them out at a local super-market, hang them on bulletin boards, and hand them to people at school. See if you can place ads in local religious bulletins, on community web sites, or in the local paper. The local paper might put you in their cal-endar of events for free or even write an article about your event! Take all the publicity you can get. You need to get the word out, so you can get the money in! But whether you make posters, hand out flyers, or put ads in the paper, make sure you list when, where, and why you are having the fund-raiser.

Sending the Money to Your Charity

There are several good ways to get money to a charity. NEVER send cash—it's just not safe in the mail.

Mailing a check. Since you probably don't have a check-book yourself, give your cash to your parents and ask them to write a check for you. Write a letter to your organization explaining what your donation is for, fold it around the check, and seal it in an envelope. You can call your charity to find out where to mail your donation, or you can check the web site for an address.

Mailing a money order. Go to the post office yourself with your cash and buy a "money order" for the amount you want to give. A money order is like a check from the post office. You give them your money, and they write the money order. There is a small fee for a money order. You may want to request a return receipt if you send money this way.

Paying by credit card. Many web sites offer the chance to donate online—using a credit card. You probably don't have credit cards yourself yet, but maybe you can ask a parent to work with you on this. If you give your parent the amount you wish to donate, they may let you use their credit card to charge that amount on the charity's web site. The charity gets your donation through the credit card, and your parent gets paid by you. If you donate this way, allow the cardholder to help you. Make sure the web site you are using is a secure site. You'll see a little lock on the bottom right-hand side of the screen if the web site is secure.

If You Are Donating Money from Donors

If you raised money simply by asking for donations, you will need to wait until the "due date" you gave donors to mail the money in. If you wrote letters or called, those donations will take time to reach your home. Keep a list of donors and how much they gave. Then you can put all the donations and the list in an envelope and send them in to your organization! You may want to include a letter to your organization explaining why you raised the money and how much

It's an Honor!

Have you ever thought about giving money in honor of someone else? A special occasion, like a birthday or anniversary, is a great opportunity for this. You can make your donation and tell the charity that it is in honor of that person's birthday. You might even be able to give an amount that lets the charity do something specific—plant one tree, for example. Some charities will send you a card that you can give to the person; if not, you can certainly get the person a regular greeting card (or make one!) and use it to write a message explaining your donation.

Another way to give in someone else's honor is to give in the memory of someone who has died. If you have lost a family member who suffered from cancer, you might choose to donate to a cancer-related charity—or to a different charity that you think your relative would have supported. To find out how to make a donation in someone's memory, call the charity or check their web site.

its work means to you. If you are given a cash dona-tion, don't mail it in. Ask a grown-up to exchange the cash for a check. Whether it's your money or someone else's money, it's always a safer option to send checks in the mail.

You should follow up with thank-you notes to your donors. Thank-you notes make donors feel good about their act—and they should! Also, your kindness may influence your donors to give again NEXT time you ask. Your organization will most likely also follow up with a thank-you note—and offer your donors a chance to "write off" their donation on their taxes.

If You Are Donating Money from Sponsors

If you raised money by participating in a sponsored event, you have a few different options. Most organizations want this to be as easy as possible—for good reasons. They will usually provide guidelines to help you.

Sometimes, you just need to mail in your sign-up sheet with your sponsors' names, addresses, and pledge amounts. The organization will then bill the sponsors, and the sponsors can pay the charity directly.

Other organizations require that you contact your

sponsors after the event to let them know how much they owe. Then, the sponsors give you a check. You can mail it following the guidelines that the organization provides.

If You Are Donating Money from a Fund-raiser

Maybe you raised money by holding your own fund-raiser. Even if you contacted the organization while you were planning the event, you should still write them a letter after it's done to go along with your donation. The letter should explain how you raised the money and just what their work means to you.

Fund-raisers often raise donations in the form of cash—you'll need to find a grown-up who will write a check for you or get a money order at a post office.

Fund-raisers don't lend themselves to keeping a list of who gave what. That means that your donors won't be getting a thank-you note from your organization—and maybe not even from you. Instead, you need to be extra appreciative on the day of the fund-raiser, so that donors know how much their gift means to you and your cause.

No Matter What Kind of Money You Are Donating

Turning in the money to your charity really is its own reward. It feels wonderful to have taken action, instead of sitting back and feeling bad about a problem. When you think about how much hard work you did—whether it was making the effort to save a little bit of your allowance each week or organizing a successful fund-raising event, you have a right to be very proud of your accomplishment.

However, sometimes there are other rewards. Your organization may send you a thank-you letter or membership materials. You may get a T-shirt or another small gift. In addition to these perks, many organizations will begin sending you reminders to give again. Now that they know what you are capable of, they're glad to have you fighting on their side!

Fundraiser Worksheet

Name of Charity

Type of Event

Date, Time, and Location

Permissions Needed

Names/Contact Info of Volunteers

Volunteers' Schedule

Publicity Plans

- O Newspapers
- O Flyers
- O TV/Radio Ads
- O School Announcements
- O Others ....

Pre-event Tasks

Event Tasks

Expenses

Earnings (Proceeds)

how do I contribute?
(Part 2)
By giving THINGS!
(all about charity drives)

Maybe you aren't interested in giving money. You would rather give an item—something physical that people can put to use, like food or clothes or toys. Instead of sending money to an organization to let them purchase things for people in need, you want to purchase those things and send them directly, so you know exactly what is going where. Or maybe you don't have any money to give or to spend—but you do have useful things around your home that you don't need anymore. You can put them to use by giving them to someone who does need them! That's the whole point of a charity drive.

What Is a Charity Drive?

A charity drive is a group effort to collect things for people in need. Usually, charity drives are run by an organization. They ask people to donate items by dropping them off at one or more specific locations. At the end of the drive, an employee or volunteer from the organization collects the donated goods. Then they sort them out and distribute them to people who need them.

There are several different types of charity drives. Here are a few you should know about.

Local drives. Many drives are run by local groups. They collect items from neighbors to help people who live in the same town, area, or state.

National drives. Large national drives collect goods from people throughout the country. Then the organizers ship the donations to a local charity office in a disadvantaged area. The local office is in charge of getting the supplies to people who need them.

International drives. Charity drives for international causes can be huge, with donations coming from generous people in many countries. An organization has to be very large to send these donations by ship or plane to a needy country overseas.

Holiday drives. Many charity drives take place during the holiday season. That's when many people feel especially thankful for the things they have . . . and more aware that not everyone is as lucky as they are. Toy drives are especially common during the holidays. Organizers ask people to drop off new toys for children who may otherwise not get any presents. Food drives are also common, especially around Thanksgiving. Organizers ask people to donate groceries that will go to a homeless shelter or to families that can't otherwise afford a festive holiday dinner.

Emergency drives. Other drives take place because of natural disasters or other emergencies. Hurricanes, tornadoes, floods, and earthquakes can cause terrible devastation. So can a fire that destroys a family's home. Events like these leave people (and animals, too!) in need of basic supplies. When a tsunami destroyed whole islands in South Asia in 2004, people lost everything. People around the globe gave millions of dollars to help. But in the days and weeks right after the tsunami, people didn't need money so much as they needed supplies: food, medicine, clothing, and materials for building shelters. Drives are a great way to help gather these things in an emergency and get them to people who need them.

How Drives Work

Drives can work in a lot of different ways. The best way to collect items depends on what items are being collected; the best way to distribute them depends on who needs them.

For example: Your local grocery store could hold a year-round pet food drive for an animal shelter. All year long, they ask you to buy some dog or cat food while you shop and drop it in a collection box on your way out of the store. Whenever the box gets full, a representative from the animal shelter comes and collects the food.

In the fall, many organizations have coat drives. They ask you to donate coats that you've outgrown or no longer use. They collect these coats and hand them out to families who don't have enough money to buy their own.

A Disaster Relief Checklist

The next time there's a natural disaster, why not put together a care package or donate to a relief drive? Here are some items that are usually needed:

○ **Food and drinks**
The food needs to be the kind that can be stored for a long time without going bad, like canned foods or dry goods. The same is true for drinks—bottled water is always good.

○ **Clothing**

○ **Baby supplies**
Disposable diapers, bottles, and formula

○ **Games, toys, and books for children**

○ **Flashlights and batteries**

○ **Sheets and blankets**

○ **Special heat blankets**
The kind that have foil on one side; you can usually buy them at any store that sells camping goods or car safety items.

○ **Pet food and travel crates**

○ **Tools**

○ **Toilet paper, soap, shampoo, and other toiletries**

Holiday toy drives may assign a specific needy child to each donor. For example, you may be told that you should purchase something that a six-year-old boy would like. It's up to you to decide what present to purchase and donate for that child. Other drives are even more specific. Some groups have each donor pick an ornament from a Christmas tree. Each ornament is marked with the name, age, and Christmas wish of one needy child. Participants in this kind of drive are asked to purchase and donate that exact item for that specific child.

New or Used?

Do you need to buy something new for a drive, or can you donate something you already own? That depends on what the drive is for. For example, you should buy a new item to donate to a toy drive; it's not often these children

"It is so neat to send things to someone in another country. You can just imagine their excitement when they get a box of clothes or food." –Kaycee, age 12

get their own toys. But at a coat drive, new or used coats are accepted for donation as long as they are clean and in good condition. For a food drive, you can either buy new food or give food you have at home (unopened, of course!). If you're unsure about what is appropriate for a drive you'd like to give to, ask!

What if the drive does allow you to give things you already own? Look around your house. Do you have any clothes that no longer fit? Any coats or shoes you no longer wear? What you consider old may feel new to someone else. Often, people keep clothes much longer than they need to. They feel guilty getting rid of something they paid for. But giving it to someone who needs it isn't really "getting rid of it." It's putting it to use again. Maybe you have a sweater you once liked and think you MAY like it again, someday. In the meantime, there are people who don't have extra clothes. And if you feel that strongly about an item, imagine how happy that item could make someone else who doesn't have many nice clothes.

Drives are great. They provide immediate relief to those in need of food, warmth, toiletries, or joy. Unlike donations of money, your item will move from your hands into the hands of someone who needs it. Many people find this way of giving more satisfying than giving money. They like the idea of shopping for an item and putting thought into their purchase. They like knowing their gift will help someone and maybe even touch their heart.

Hosting a Charity Drive

Now that you know all about charity drives, you might want to plan one yourself! As always, start by contacting the organization you want your efforts to benefit; they may have instructions and rules for you to follow. They may also be able to help you.

You can host a drive that lasts several weeks or just one day. For example, maybe you will collect used coats from Thanksgiving until New Year's Day. Or you can publicize a one-day drive where people can donate toys—on

Two-for-One

Giving used items is special because it lets you share the joy an item has given you. But there's a second reason to feel great about donating something used: it's good for the environment! You are reusing and recycling goods. Your one thoughtful act helps two causes.

the day after Christmas. You may decide to hold a book drive on March 2nd, Dr. Seuss's birthday and the day that the National Education Association has designated as "Read Across America" day.

Whichever you choose, the supplies you need are very simple: some posters and flyers, some storage boxes, and two or three friends. You can publicize by telling people, putting ads in papers, or hanging signs on local bulletin boards. If your drive requires people to bring items from home (like books or used coats), make sure you publicize your drive well in advance. Each time they pass a sign or see an ad, potential donors will be reminded of your drive. If you host a one-day drive, this is particularly important.

Don't forget to spread the news by word of mouth, too. Talk to local businesses, families, friends, and neighbors.

Are there things you can do to make it easy for people to donate? For example, can you pick up donations at people's homes, so they don't have to bring their items to you? If so, let people know! (And make sure to bring a grown-up with you when you pick up donations from strangers.) Many potential donors who have lots to give don't bother because they think it is inconvenient. By making it easy for them, you can turn a non-donor into someone who loves to give!

Once you've spread the word that you'll be having a drive, you need to find a location to host your drive. A good place to have a drive is one with lots of people traffic. For example, a train station is a perfect place for a coat drive. A library is a logical place for a book drive. A food drive? Try a grocery store. Think of a busy place that relates to your theme. You'll need to work with a train-station or store manager or whoever is in charge of your location. This is especially true if your drive lasts more than one day. You'll want to be in contact with someone who can be there every day and let you know if you need to come by and pick up a filled box. Most of the time, store owners are glad to help—your charitable cause means more sales for them! Think about it—if you want to collect food for an animal shelter, a pet store would be glad to place a box near the front of their store. People could see the box on the way in and buy extra supplies from their store. You win, the store wins—and the pets win!

Hosting a one-day drive requires a little more work. For starters, you need to work extra hard on publicizing your drive. You want people to know about the drive—so that people can plan to come with dona-

Minding Your Manners

Whether someone agrees to donate an item or not, always remember to be polite. Of course, you know to thank donors who give you money or items; tell them how much their gift will mean to your cause and to you. But don't judge people who decide not to give. Remember that you don't know anyone's situation. They may not be able to give a gift, or they may already donate a lot to other charitable causes. Thank them for their time anyway. Being polite means you can go back and ask for another donation in the future.

tions. On the day of the drive, arrive early to set up. Place signs where people can see them. With a friend or two, let passersby know that you are collecting for your cause. When you begin to get donations, make sure others can see them. This will encourage them to donate, too.

Once your drive is over, you will need to get your goods to the organization you are working with. Maybe a parent will volunteer to drive you and your goods to a local shelter—but it may take more than one trip! Larger organizations, like Goodwill, may be

"I have done lots of research on the medical supply needs in third world countries, and it amazes me how little other countries have. I am going to do an Eagle Scout project to gather and send supplies to countries that don't even have Band-Aids." –Nicholas, age 14

willing to pick up your donations at a pre-arranged time. Either way, you need to arrange for transportation of your goods before the drive begins!

At the end of the drive, don't forget to clean up your supplies and thank the contact with whom you've been working at your location. Drives can be exhausting! But they give you that good kind of tired—the kind that comes from doing something really worthwhile!

Charity Drive Worksheet

Name of Charity

Goods to Be Donated

Where People Can Donate

Permissions Needed

Names/Contact Info of Volunteers

Volunteers' Schedule

Publicity Plans

- O Newspapers
- O Flyers
- O TV/Radio Ads
- O School Announcements
- O Others ....

Pre-drive Tasks

Drive Tasks

Expenses

NOTES

CHAPTER 5

how do I contribute? (Part 3)

By giving your TIME AND EFFORT!

Maybe your idea of giving is different than any we've mentioned. Giving money or things are nice options—but for many people, neither provides enough involvement. Rather than giving something, they would rather be in the middle of the action doing something to make a real difference.

If this sounds like you, why not try volunteering? Volunteering really involves you in the situation. You physically step into the problem and help solve it. All you have to do is give your time and effort to a good cause. Then you're doing something AND giving something. For many people, that kind of charity feels better than giving in other ways. Volunteering is the best way to immediately see the difference you make.

Kids make great volunteers. You have more energy than most adults—and more skills than you get credit for. Every day, you balance school, homework, after-school activities, siblings, helping around the house, helping at dinner . . . and somehow you still find time to have fun. Balancing all those things takes energy and skills. And as a kid, you are used to learning how to do new things all the time. No matter what your charitable cause is, your energy, skills, and willingness to learn are needed and will be appreciated.

Volunteering is also great for kids because it usually doesn't cost any money. No one will charge you to volunteer. Usually, you don't need to buy equipment or pay to take classes. All you need to donate as a volunteer is time and your willingness to work!

"When I helped a younger kid get second place in a wheelchair race, it felt good just to see the reaction on his face at the finish line." –Peter James, age 14

What You Get Back

When you give by volunteering, you get back a lot, too. Here are just a few of the perks!

You gain confidence. When you volunteer, you will find out how much your contributions matter to others, to the cause you're helping, and to the other volunteers on your team. Even if you are new and just learning what to do, you are an important part of the effort. Each time you volunteer, you'll get more experienced—and more valuable to the team. That's a lot to be proud of.

You learn new skills. Volunteering gives you the chance to learn new skills you can use throughout life. Working at a soup kitchen can teach you skills that are useful if you want to try cooking at home or working as a party helper for a caterer. If you volunteer to help fix up a local park or playground in your town, you'll learn a lot about gardening and landscaping. Volunteering to walk dogs at a shelter gives you skills that are useful if you want to earn some spare cash by running a dog-walking service. It will also help if you decide to work at a zoo or as a vet someday.

You get to do activities you enjoy. There's no reason you can't choose volunteer jobs that let you do some of your favorite activities. If you love painting, volunteer to paint a mural in a disadvantaged school. If you love soccer, volunteer to spend the day teaching soccer to kids who don't have other opportunities to learn. If you love building things, volunteer to help fix up a run-down community center. Volunteering to do something you love is a win-win situation.

It opens your eyes to other people. When you volunteer, you'll meet people who may seem very different from you—different in age, race, nationality, religion, or amount of money they have. But you'll be amazed to find out how much you have in common! Start by looking at the other volunteers. No matter what your differences are, at heart you all have the same goal. You are all caring and brave enough to give your own time to make the world a better place.

You have a lot in common with the people you are helping, too. A kid living in a shelter or eating in a soup kitchen may seem worlds away from you—but he may admire the same sports star, have the same pet peeves, or dislike the same subjects in school. An elderly woman you visit in a nursing home may seem at first to have nothing in common with you—but take the time to talk, and you may find that she loves the same TV shows and laughs at the same jokes you do.

Meeting people whose lives are very different from yours—and discovering that you have a lot in common with them—is not only a perk of volunteering . . . it's also a reminder of why volunteering matters. It's a reminder that we are all connected: the young and the old, the healthy and the ill, the rich and the poor. We are all part of the same world, the same big family. Working to help people who aren't as lucky as you are is a good reminder that they are still part of your community.

Volunteering lets you see the world in a new way. Suppose you join Habitat for Humanity, an organization that builds homes, parks, and playgrounds in communities that need them. You might discover that there are parts of your town where families are in need of new homes. Or suppose you get your parent's permission to go on a midnight run to give out food or blankets to homeless people on a cold night. Would you be shocked to see homeless people in your own town—spending their nights sleeping in the doorway of your favorite store?

Some volunteers even get to visit faraway places around the world! Philanthropic vacations are trips that you take with your family to do charity work. You might dig a well in rural Africa, help build a school in Latin America, or build libraries in villages in Tibet. These trips are usually organized by a company or a non-profit organization that knows the area well.

No matter where you go, you'll never look at your life (or the world) the same way again. You'll realize that the world is a very big place, with more variety than you ever imagined. You'll also learn that all the things you thought were "normal"—watching TV, living in a heated house or apartment with your parents and siblings, buying food at a supermarket—are normal only in the part of the world you come from. Many people in the world live happy, satisfied lives even though they have less money, less "stuff," and less comfort than you're used to. And you'll learn firsthand about people who have so little that their lives are a constant struggle.

Finding a Deeper Connection

The biggest reward of volunteering is that it touches you in a way that no other experience can. Seeing a TV news report or reading about suffering is nothing compared to seeing the problem up close and helping to relieve it.

You may wonder: how can feeling bad be called a perk? Feeling bad is no fun! But feeling bad and developing the strength to overcome it and make a difference is great. It makes you a stronger person, with a deeper connection to the world you live in. And that is an amazing perk.

Volunteering can be incredibly exciting if you choose a cause that you care about and a type of volunteering that suits your personality. There are so many opportunities out there; you're bound to find one that's right for you.

Making Your Own Opportunities to Help

You may think that you need to be part of some organization in order to help out. Not true! If you look closely around your local community, you will find something or someone in need of help. Here are some ideas.

Show a younger student "the ropes" at your school. If your school doesn't have a mentoring program, why not start one? Talk to your principal! You never know who needs someone to look up to.

Tutor younger students for free. Ask your teacher to put up a poster in the teacher's lounge. Teachers have the best idea of who needs the kind of help you have to offer.

Visit the elderly in a nursing home. You can stop by or call the nursing home's front desk to ask how. Do you play piano? Offer to put on a show! Do you enjoy writing? Offer to help write letters for those who can no longer do it themselves.

Make time for an older relative who lives alone. You can visit them once a week—offer to do chores or just sit with them. If you're far away, why not call or write them once a week?

Help a disabled neighbor. Vision-impaired people might like someone to read aloud to them; people who can't move around easily might appreciate your help in running errands. If you don't know anyone, ask trusted adults if they know someone who might be able to use your help. You may be surprised at how very many people close to you know someone in need.

Be Sensitive

Sometimes, people have a hard time accepting charity. Often, those who most need charity don't even like the sound of the word. Isn't it sometimes hard to admit you need help? If you have a neighbor who can't get around easily, you need to be sensitive with your approach. "I was just on my way to the store and thought I'd stop by and see if I could pick up anything for you. Need anything?" is MUCH better than, "I thought I'd stop by and see if I could shop for you, because you can't do it that well"—or, worse, "I really want to do some charity, so I have decided to help you!"

And don't give up easily. Sometimes people are slow to accept help—but keep asking every so often. People don't want to make someone else go out of their way. So, when you offer help, no matter what kind of help you're offering, make sure you seem like the task is on your way or would be enjoyable to you. That will make your neighbors or relatives feel better about accepting your help.

Clean up your neighborhood or local playground. You don't have to wait for someone else to organize a big event. Grab a trash bag and some heavy gloves and get to work! If you get some friends to help you, you can have a lot of fun. However, be sure to ask your parents for permission first.

Help at home. Helping someone close to you is just as important as helping those you don't know. Does your mother work and take care of the house? Why not give her a book of coupons: "Good for one day of gardening," "Good for dinner one night," "Good for one night of baby-sitting." Being charitable toward your family (or a friend) doesn't require a special occasion. Charitable acts just require you to go out of your way a little more than you already do.

Opportunities with Local Organizations

Because they're smaller, local charities often need your help more than huge national or international groups do. They may also be more likely to give you interesting work that lets you roll up your sleeves and really get your hands dirty! Here are a few ways to get involved.

If you are concerned about saving dolphins, you can volunteer at a local aquarium. You'll be able to see what goes on behind the scenes. And you can learn about and see dolphins every time you visit.

If you are concerned about stray cats and dogs, volunteer at your local shelter. They may even let you walk dogs or "socialize" (play with) kittens. If your parents agree, you could even foster an animal. That means you will give it a temporary home until someone else adopts it for good. This saves the animal from living in the shelter. It also makes room in the shelter for another animal on the streets.

If you are concerned about world hunger, you might think you need to join a group that helps feed starving people around the globe. But your local soup kitchen needs help, too—there are hungry people living near you right now! You could also check out Meals on Wheels, an organization that brings food and groceries to the disabled. They may be able to set you up with a neighbor who would love a warm meal delivered to the door. You can find a local branch of this organization on their web site, www.mowaa.org.

"It felt amazing to help, like being a superhero. I was surprised to at how much help people needed." –Lauren, age 13

Opportunities with National or Global Charities

National or global charities often do work that is strictly "adults only." Many of the grown-ups who work with these charities devote their entire lives to their cause. But that doesn't mean the groups don't have ways that kids like you can help. Here are a few examples.

Greenpeace is known for its environmental work around the world. One of its most famous ways of protesting whale hunting is to send volunteers out to sea in an inflatable raft to block the path of a huge whaling ship. The volunteers hold up signs protesting the hunt from their little raft. It's a dangerous mission. Only adults can go. But as a kid, you could help their cause by stuffing envelopes with news of the latest victory. You may even be able to pass out buttons or flyers. That might not seem as exciting as floating on a raft out at sea . . . but it's still a very important job! Charities like Greenpeace rely on volunteers to help get the word out about their activities.

The Peace Corps is another famous organization that sends volunteers to locations around the world. Wherever volunteers are sent, they are required to stay for several years, helping the local community by doing things like teaching, farming, or building. To be chosen as a Peace

Corps volunteer, you'll need lots of important skills—speaking foreign languages, knowing something about farming, being an experienced builder . . . It all depends on where you are going. It also helps to have done a lot of volunteering before you apply. So, if you'd like to help the Peace Corps build a community one day, start volunteering now! Help build a park, or clean polluted areas. Getting experience under your belt will help you develop skills needed by the Peace Corps. By the time you are old enough to enter the Peace Corps, you'll be ready: you'll know exactly what you want to do and where you want to go.

Getting Started

Finding a place to volunteer is not hard at all. Most newspapers have a section that calls for volunteers. Your local town hall or religious organization can tell you the names of several local charities. Web sites can be helpful, too. You can visit web sites like www.idealist.org, which lists several thousand volunteer opportunities. You can search by state and town.

Although many of the listings you'll find are for adults, some will be open to kids. If you don't find an opportunity that suits you, you still may learn how to contact an organization that works on your favorite cause. Or maybe you already know about an organization you want to help, but don't know how. Go ahead—call them, e-mail them, or write them a letter! If you show your enthusiasm, they may be able to create a perfect opportunity just for you.

Once you've found your opportunity, how do you decide how much time you can give? You can offer only as much time as you have free. You might decide to volunteer once a week, or you might want to try volunteering for just a one-day event. Chances are, if you volunteer once, you'll see how much you mean to your organization. You'll see the difference that you made, and you'll want to help again . . . and again!

NOTES

A Final Word From Freddi Zeiler

This book contains just a small fraction of the world's great non-profit organizations, because I couldn't have possibly fit them all in here. So don't feel limited to the charities I've listed. Instead, use them as a place to start. Read about these charities, and if you realize that you're interested in something that I haven't included or are just curious to see what else is out there, do some detective work of your own. Maybe you want to help out a local charity. Or maybe you have a friend or family member affected by a certain disease or disorder and want to give to an organization that deals specifically with that issue. Contributing your time, money, or goods to a cause that means something to you is really important.

There are lots of other wonderful organizations that I have yet to discover, but that doesn't mean you can't do it on your own. So here are some tips that I used to choose which charities I wanted to help: First, I recommend that you find a charity search engine. I used several different ones for my research. What they do is help match people to charities that suit their interests. You can search by name, subject, rating, and even location. These are my personal favorites:

www.charitynavigator.org

www.guidestar.org

www.give.org

www.charitywatch.org

Second, almost every non-profit organization has a web site, and they often give you all the information you need. Web sites are a valuable tool in learning about charities. Third, you can use the same categories that I did as guidelines to organize the information, or, if there are other categories you feel are important, come up with your own list. Determine what you think is most important in a charity and find one that meets those requirements. The more committed you are to a cause, the more rewarding your contribution will be.

I hope that the following charities inspire you, as they did me. They are some of my favorite organizations, and all are devoted, just like you are, to making the world a better place.

NOTES

Adopt-a-Minefield
American Cancer Society
American Civil Liberties Union
American Diabetes Association
American Heart Association
American Humane Association
American Legacy Foundation
American National Red Cross
AmeriCares
Amfar
Amnesty International USA
Believe in Tomorrow National
   Children's Foundation
CARE
Childhelp
Children's Defense Fund
Children's HeartLink
Cystic Fibrosis Foundation
Direct Relief International
Doctors Without Borders
Elizabeth Glaser Pediatric
   AIDS Foundation
Equality Now

Give Kids The World
Goodwill Industries International
Habitat for Humanity
Heifer International
Human Rights Watch
International Rescue Committee
Lance Armstrong Foundation
Make-A-Wish Foundation International
March of Dimes
Meals on Wheels
National Center for Missing
   & Exploited Children
Orphan Foundation of America
Project HOPE
Save the Children
SOS Children's Villages
Stand for Children
The Susan G. Komen Breast
   Cancer Foundation
UNICEF, the United Nations
   Children's Fund
United Negro College Fund

Adopt-a-Minefield

What is the organization's mission?

To eliminate the threat of landmines by clearing minefields, helping landmine survivors, and supporting a ban on the use of landmines.

How will the organization spend my money?

It works to clear minefields, develop national capacity in mine-affected countries, and return land to productive use. It also raises money to help those injured by landmines and educate the public about its cause.

Break it down!

One hundred percent of every dollar you contribute goes directly to mine-removal programs, because the management is supported by outside organizations like The Better World Fund.

Anything else I should know?

How much money does it take to clear an entire minefield? Usually from about $25,000 to $40,000! But no worries, Adopt-a-Minefield is happy with any size contribution, which will go directly to the cause.

How can I donate or get more information on this charity?

Internet: www.landmines.org
Email: info@landmines.org
Phone: (212) 907-1305
Fax: (212) 682-9185
Mail: UNA-USA, 801 Second Avenue, New York, NY 10017

American Cancer Society

What is the organization's mission?

To eliminate cancer as a major health problem by preventing cancer, saving lives, and diminishing suffering from cancer, through research, education, advocacy, and service.

How will the organization spend my money?

To fund research, provide cancer information services, provide community programs aimed at reducing cancer risk and detecting cancer as early as possible, and provide cancer advocacy.

Break it down!

Seventy-one cents out of every dollar go toward the programs. Seven cents go to running the organization and 22 cents go to fund-raising.

Anything else I should know?

The American Cancer Society also offers programs to help educate the public about cancer risks, early detection methods, and prevention.

How can I donate or get more information on this charity?

Internet: www.cancer.org
Email: through web site
Phone: (800) 227-2345
Fax: none
Mail: P.O. Box 22718, Oklahoma City, OK 73123

American Civil Liberties Union (ACLU)

What is the organization's mission?

To protect individual rights. It focuses specifically on freedom of speech, freedom of religion, equal treatment under the law, and a right for privacy.

How will the organization spend my money?

The ACLU goes to court in civil liberties cases to defend the Bill of Rights. It also educates the public.

Break it down!

Just over 78 cents of every dollar go to the programs, while 12 cents is for management, and 10 cents is for fund-raising.

Anything else I should know?

The ACLU deals with more than 6,000 court cases every year!

How can I donate or get more information on this charity?

Internet: www.aclu.org
Email: aclu@aclu.org
Phone: (212) 549-2500
Fax: none
Mail: 125 Broad Street, 18th Floor, New York, NY 10004

American Diabetes Association

What is the organization's mission?

To prevent and cure diabetes and to improve the lives of all people affected by diabetes.

How will the organization spend my money?

The money raised by the association funds research, information programs, and advocacy efforts that support more than 20 million people with diabetes in communities across America.

Break it down!

Seventy-eight cents out of every dollar go toward the programs. Four cents go to running the organization and 18 cents go to fund-raising.

Anything else I should know?

The American Diabetes Association is the nation's leading non-profit health organization providing diabetes research, information, and advocacy. Founded in 1940, the association conducts programs in all 50 states and the District of Columbia, reaching hundreds of communities.

How can I donate or get more information on this charity?

Internet: www.diabetes.org
Email: through web site
Phone: (888) 700-7029
Fax: (703) 683-1839
Mail: P.O. Box 7023, Merrifield, VA 22116

American Heart Association

What is the organization's mission?

To reduce the number of people disabled or killed by heart disease and strokes.

How will the organization spend my money?

The organization works to prevent disease, detect it, and treat it. Donations go to many different programs, such as medical care, searching for organ donors, and education.

Break it down!

Almost 77 cents of every dollar go straight to the programs. Eight cents is for administration costs and 15 for fund-raising.

Anything else I should know?

Heart disease is America's number one killer and strokes are number three.

How can I donate or get more information on this charity?

Internet: www.americanheart.org
Email: walter.bristol@heart.org
Phone: (800) 242-8721
Fax: none
Mail: 7272 Greenville Avenue, Dallas, TX 75231

American Humane Association

What is the organization's mission?

To prevent cruelty, abuse, neglect, and exploitation of children and animals and to assure that their interests and well-being are fully, effectively, and humanely guaranteed by an aware and caring society.

How will the organization spend my money?

For animals, it helps shelters across the country with things such as adoption programs, sanitation, and education. It offers emergency animal relief efforts in areas affected by disasters. For children, it provides public outreach through education and training to improve children's welfare and prevent maltreatment.

Break it down!

About 85 cents of every dollar go directly to the services. Around six cents go to administration and about nine cents to fund-raising.

Anything else I should know?

The American Humane Association was started in 1877 and is the country's only non-profit organization that protects both children and animals.

How can I donate or get more information on this charity?

Internet: www.americanhumane.org
Email: through web site
Phone: (303) 792-9900
Fax: (303) 792-5333
Mail: 63 Inverness Drive East, Englewood, CO 80112

American Legacy Foundation

What is the organization's mission?

To create a world in which young people reject tobacco and anyone can quit.

How will the organization spend my money?

It is involved in programs to prevent youth from smoking and help adults to quit. It does this most famously through the "truth" advertising campaign.

Break it down!

About 88 cents of every dollar go to program expenses, while 12 cents go to management.

Anything else I should know?

In 2002, the "truth" campaign reduced the number of young smokers by 300,000.

How can I donate or get more information on this charity?

Internet: www.americanlegacy.org
Email: info@americanlegacy.org
Phone: (202) 454-5555
Fax: (202) 454-5599
Mail: 2030 M Street, NW, Sixth Floor, Washington, DC 20036

American National Red Cross

What is the organization's mission?

To provide aid for people struck by natural disasters; to prevent and prepare for emergencies; to save lives and relieve suffering in the United States and internationally.

How will the organization spend my money?

Your money goes to work in disaster relief, health and safety training, and managing nearly half of the United States' blood supply.

Break it down!

About 91 cents of every dollar go to programs and services. The other nine cents is used for management and fund-raising.

Anything else I should know?

You can donate your pocket change to the American Red Cross at Coinstar machines now! Just bring your change with you to the supermarket.

How can I donate or get more information on this charity?

Internet: www.redcross.org
Email: through web site
Phone: (800) 435-7669 to make a donation;
(202) 303-4498 for information
Fax: none
Mail: P.O. Box 37243, Washington, DC 20013 to make a donation; 2025 E Street, NW, Washington, DC 20006 for information

AmeriCares

What is the organization's mission?

To provide immediate response to emergency medical needs in the wake of disasters, and to support long-term humanitarian assistance programs for people in need around the world.

How will the organization spend my money?

AmeriCares asks companies to donate medicine, medical supplies, and other relief materials, and gives them to international health care organizations and welfare providers. Your donation will be used to ship or airlift supplies to those in need or to buy materials that are in urgent need and can't be donated.

Break it down!

Almost 99 cents of every dollar go directly to helping others! Thanks to so many volunteers and donations, only one cent goes towards fund-raising and managing the programs.

Anything else I should know?

Since it began, this organization has contributed over $5 billion in aid to more than 137 countries.

How can I donate or get more information on this charity?

Internet: www.americares.org
Email: communications@americares.org
Phone: (800) 486-4357
Fax: (203) 327-5200
Mail: 88 Hamilton Avenue, Stamford, CT 06902

Amfar

What is the organization's mission?

To promote AIDS research; AIDS prevention, treatment, and education; and advocacy of AIDS-related public policy.

How will the organization spend my money?

They work on many different levels to combat HIV, focusing on prevention, advocacy, education, and research.

Break it down!

Almost 78 cents of every dollar go straight to the programs. Out of the remaining change, seven cents go to management and 15 to fund-raising.

Anything else I should know?

It has put over $233 million toward fighting HIV/AIDS since it began in 1985.

How can I donate or get more information on this charity?

Internet: www.amfar.org
Email: info@amfar.org
Phone: (212) 806-1600
Fax: (212) 806-1601
Mail: 120 Wall Street, 13th Floor, New York, NY 10005-3908

Amnesty International USA

What is the organization's mission?

To protect and promote the human rights of people around the globe.

How will the organization spend my money?

Amnesty International's vision is of a world in which every person enjoys all human rights. Its work focuses on preventing and ending grave abuses of the human rights of all people, including ending torture, the death penalty, discrimination, and other forms of punishment or abuse that go against basic human rights.

Break it down!

Seventy-seven cents of your dollar go to the programs, three cents to management, and 20 cents to fund-raising.

Anything else I should know?

They have more than 1.8 million members in over 150 countries and territories in every region of the world.

How can I donate or get more information on this charity?

Internet: www.amnestyusa.org
Email: aimember@aiusa.org
Phone: (212) 807-8400 for information;
(800) 266-3789 to make a donation
Fax: (212) 627-1451
Mail: 5 Penn Plaza, New York, NY 10001

Believe in Tomorrow National Children's Foundation

What is the organization's mission?

To help relieve the stress and strain that children (and their families) feel when they are being treated for a life-threatening disease.

How will the organization spend my money?

It creates and runs educational programs, recreational programs, and support services for ill children and their families to help "ease pain, reduce loneliness, and bring joy to children throughout their treatment process."

Break it down!

About 92 cents of every dollar raised go directly toward providing programs and services. The other eight cents go to administrative and general costs.

Anything else I should know?

This charity sponsors one-day "adventures" for sick children, such as spending the day at the racetrack as honorary pit-crew members, flying in a blimp, or meeting bull riders at the rodeo.

How can I donate or get more information on this charity?

Internet: www.believeintomorrow.org
Email: through web site
Phone: (800) 933-5470
Fax: (410) 744-1984
Mail: 6601 Frederick Road, Baltimore, MD 21228

CARE

What is the organization's mission?

To fight poverty in areas that need it most, provide aid, and promote awareness of global issues.

How will the organization spend my money?

CARE uses donations to provide emergency relief, agricultural training, health care, clean water, education projects, and economic opportunities in the poorest parts of the world. It also uses donations to strengthen its political voice and to bring international issues to the attention of policy makers.

Break it down!

Ninety-one cents of every dollar go towards program activities. Nine cents go toward administrative and fund-raising expenditures.

Anything else I should know?

CARE works with poor communities in 70 countries around the world. It places special focus on working with women because, equipped with the proper resources, women have the power to help whole families and entire communities escape poverty.

How can I donate or get more information on this charity?

Internet: www.careusa.org
Email: info@care.org
Phone: (800) 521-2273 to make a donation; (800) 422-7385 for information
Fax: (404) 589-2651
Mail: 151 Ellis St., NE, Atlanta, GA 30303

Childhelp

What is the organization's mission?

To meet the physical, emotional, educational, and spiritual needs of abused and neglected children.

How will the organization spend my money?

It helps those in need by focusing efforts and resources in the areas of treatment, prevention, and research. It runs an abuse hotline and advocacy centers, and promotes foster care, counseling, educational programs, training, and community outreach.

Break it down!

About 89 cents of every dollar go to the programs. About seven cents go towards management and four cents go towards fund-raising.

Anything else I should know?

Childhelp is one of the largest and oldest national non-profit organizations for children. Childhelp National Child Abuse Hotline (1-800-4-A-CHILD) provides 24-hour child abuse crisis counseling.

How can I donate or get more information on this charity?

Internet: www.childhelp.org
Email: none
Phone: (480) 922-8212
Fax: (480) 922-7061
Mail: 15757 N. 78th Street, Scottsdale, AR 85260

Children's Defense Fund (CDF)

What is the organization's mission?

To Leave No Child Behind and to ensure every child a Healthy Start, a Head Start, a Fair Start, a Safe Start, and a Moral Start in life and successful passage to adulthood with the help of caring families and communities. It also educates the nation about the needs of children and encourages preventive investment before children get sick, into trouble, drop out of school, or suffer family breakdown.

How will the organization spend my money?

The Children's Defense Fund provides a strong, effective voice for all the children of America who cannot vote, lobby, or speak for themselves. CDF trains young leaders, operates literacy-rich Freedom Schools for disadvantaged children, and provides scholarships to high school youth who have "beaten the odds" through its Beat the Odds scholarship program.

Break it down!

Almost 84 cents of every dollar go towards protecting children. Five cents is put towards fund-raisers and the remaining 11 cents to management.

How can I donate or get more information on this charity?

Internet: www.childrensdefense.org
Email: cdfinfo@childrensdefense.org
Phone: (800) 233-1200
Fax: (202) 662-3510
Mail: 25 E Street NW, Washington, DC 20001

Children's HeartLink

What is the organization's mission?

To improve how children's heart disease is prevented and treated in developing countries.

How will the organization spend my money?

HeartLink sends medical teams and supplies to communities in need. It also trains members of the community, so that they can help themselves in the future.

Break it down!

About 63 cents of each dollar go to support program services and 16 cents go to fund-raising. Eleven cents go to running the organization.

Anything else I should know?

HeartLink has helped children with heart disease in 35 different countries and given more than $55 million worth of aid since it began in 1969.

How can I donate or get more information on this charity?

Internet: www.childrensheartlink.org
Email: info@childrensheartlink.org
Phone: (952) 928-4860
Fax: (952) 928-4859
Mail: 5075 Arcadia Avenue, Minneapolis, MN 55436

Cystic Fibrosis Foundation

What is the organization's mission?

To find ways to cure and control cystic fibrosis, and to improve the quality of life for people who have this deadly genetic lung disease.

How will the organization spend my money?

Donations go to support scientific research on the disease to help find a cure. They also support cystic fibrosis care centers for people diagnosed with CF.

Break it down!

About 85 cents of every dollar are available for cystic fibrosis research and care programs.

Anything else I should know?

About 30,000 children and adults in the United States live with cystic fibrosis.

How can I donate or get more information on this charity?

Internet: www.cff.org
Email: info@cff.org
Phone: (800) 344-4823
Fax: (301) 951-6378
Mail: 6931 Arlington Road, Bethesda, MD 20814

Direct Relief International

What is the organization's mission?

To improve people's lives by creating better and more access to health care around the world.

How will the organization spend my money?

The organization supports hospitals and other health care facilities in countries suffering greatly from disease, disaster, poverty, or war. It makes medicine, vitamins, and services more readily available to those in need.

Break it down!

Over 99 cents of every dollar go directly towards helping others. Less than one cent goes to administrative and fund-raising expenses.

Anything else I should know?

Direct Relief International was started in 1948. It does not associate itself with any religious or political organization and offers its help without discrimination.

How can I donate or get more information on this charity?

Internet: www.directrelief.org
Email: info@directrelief.org
Phone: (805) 964-4767
Fax: (805) 681-4838
Mail: 27 S. La Patera Lane, Santa Barbara, CA 93117

Doctors Without Borders (DWB)

What is the organization's mission?

To deliver emergency aid to people affected by armed conflict, epidemics, natural or man-made disasters, or exclusion from health care in more than 80 countries.

How will the organization spend my money?

DWB is an international, independent medical humanitarian organization that goes to troubled parts of the world and holds large-scale vaccine campaigns, trains medical staff, provides medical care, fixes hospitals, and tries to get medicine to people even if the roads are destroyed or blocked by disasters or war.

Break it down!

Eighty-six cents of every dollar go towards services.

Anything else I should know?

The organization sends volunteer doctors, nurses, water and sanitation engineers, and other experts on over 3,800 aid missions every year.

How can I donate or get more information on this charity?

Internet: www.doctorswithoutborders.org
Email: through web site
Phone: (888) 392-0392
Fax: (212) 679-7016
Mail: 333 Seventh Avenue, 2nd floor, New York, NY 10001

Elizabeth Glaser Pediatric AIDS Foundation

What is the organization's mission?

To create a future of hope for children and families worldwide by eradicating pediatric AIDS, providing care and treatment for people with HIV/AIDS, and accelerating the discovery of new treatments for other serious and life-threatening pediatric illnesses.

How will the organization spend my money?

Your money will be spent to support innovative and unparalleled research, care, treatment, and advocacy programs to lead the fight against pediatric HIV/AIDS and other serious and life-threatening diseases affecting children.

Break it down!

Around 81 cents of every dollar go to fund innovative research and implementation of programs. Eight cents go toward administration. Around 11 cents is for fund-raising.

Anything else I should know?

The foundation was started by three moms around a kitchen table after one of them, Elizabeth Glaser, contracted HIV through a blood transfusion and unknowingly passed the virus to her daughter, Ariel, and her son, Jake.

How can I donate or get more information on this charity?

Internet: www.pedaids.org
Email: info@pedaids.org
Phone: (310) 314-1459 or (888) 499-HOPE
Fax: (310) 314-1469
Mail: 2950 31st Street, Suite 125, Santa Monica, CA 90405

Equality Now

What is the organization's mission?

To protect and promote human rights of women and girls around the world.

How will the organization spend my money?

Equality Now creates awareness of human rights violations against women—including rape, domestic violence, human trafficking, and discrimination at work, school, and in the political arena—and mobilizes public pressure to end them.

Break it down!

Eighty-one cents of every dollar go straight to the program.

Anything else I should know?

Equality Now feels that human rights violations against women and girls have been overlooked in the past by governments and the media. Millions of women and girls around the world are the victims of ongoing injustice.

How can I donate or get more information on this charity?

Internet: www.equalitynow.org
Email: info@equalitynow.org
Phone: (212) 586-0906
Fax: (212) 586-1611
Mail: P.O. Box 20646, Columbus Circle Station, New York, NY 10023

Give Kids The World

What is the organization's mission?

To bring happiness to children with life-threatening illnesses and their families, by giving them a weeklong fantasy vacation.

How will the organization spend my money?

Donations support the Give Kids The World Village in Florida, where kids and their families live and eat for free during their vacation and are provided with free tickets to Orlando attractions.

Break it down!

About 92 cents of every dollar go directly to serve children and their families. The other eight cents go to fund-raising and administrative costs.

Anything else I should know?

Each year over 25,000 children are diagnosed with a life-threatening illness.

How can I donate or get more information on this charity?

Internet: www.GKTW.org
Email: dream@gktw.org
Phone: (407) 396-1114 or (800) 995-KIDS
Fax: none
Mail: 210 S. Bass Road, Kissimmee, FL 34746

Goodwill Industries International

What is the organization's mission?

To work internationally to help people help themselves; to empower those with special needs to find employment.

How will the organization spend my money?

Goodwill works to educate and train disadvantaged people (such as homeless people, poorly educated people, and people who are physically or mentally disabled) to help them start a career. Revenue from the sale of donated clothing and household items at over 2,000 Goodwill stores and at Goodwill's Internet auction site (shopgoodwill.com) helps fund the organization's goals.

Break it down!

Of every dollar raised by Goodwill, 84 cents go towards supporting Goodwill's mission. The remainder covers management costs.

Anything else I should know?

Goodwill is one of the world's biggest non-profit organizations. Last year, local Goodwills collectively provided jobs or training to more than 720,000 people.

How can I donate or get more information on this charity?

Internet: www.goodwill.org
Email: contactus@goodwill.org
Phone: (800) 741-0186
Fax: (301) 530-1516
Mail: 15810 Indianola Drive, Rockville, MD 20855

Habitat for Humanity

What is the organization's mission?

To eliminate poverty housing and homelessness from the world and to make decent shelter a matter of conscience and action.

How will the organization spend my money?

Donations are used to build houses at no profit in partnership with families.

Break it down!

Eighty-three cents of each dollar go to the programs, while nine cents is for management and general costs, and eight cents is for fund-raising.

Anything else I should know?

Habitat for Humanity is a non-profit, ecumenical Christian housing ministry that has built more than 200,000 houses around the world since it began in 1976.

How can I donate or get more information on this charity?

Internet: www.habitat.org
Email: publicinfo@habitat.org
Phone: (229) 924-6935
Fax: none
Mail: 121 Habitat Street, Americus, GA 31709

Heifer International

What is the organization's mission?

To end world hunger and poverty and to care for Earth.

How will the organization spend my money?

Heifer International provides livestock and agricultural training to families in impoverished parts of the world. It also helps communities protect themselves and recover from disasters; manage their land, livestock and natural resources; and combat HIV/AIDS.

Break it down!

Seventy-two cents of each dollar go straight to the cause; the rest goes to management and fund-raising.

Anything else I should know?

This charity believes that giving families a source of food and income (such as livestock or agriculture) is more helpful than providing short-term relief. Sixty-one years old, Heifer International has touched millions of families in 128 countries.

How can I donate or get more information on this charity?

Internet: www.heifer.org
Email: through web site
Phone: (800) 422-0474
Fax: none
Mail: P.O. Box 8058, Little Rock, AR 72203

Human Rights Watch

What is the organization's mission?

To defend human rights worldwide.

How will the organization spend my money?

Your money will go to investigating human rights abuse cases, exposing them, and finding solutions that work.

Break it down!

About 79 cents of every dollar go to the programs, while five cents go to administration, and 16 cents go to fund-raising.

Anything else I should know?

This is the largest human rights organization in the United States. It works with both the United Nations and European Union.

How can I donate or get more information on this charity?

Internet: www.hrw.org
Email: hrwnyc@hrw.org
Phone: (212) 290-4700
Fax: (212) 736-1300
Mail: 350 Fifth Avenue, 34th Floor, New York, NY 10118

International Rescue Committee

What is the organization's mission?

To offer life-saving assistance to people uprooted by war, violence, and persecution—and to help people around the world rebuild their lives.

How will the organization spend my money?

The International Rescue Committee provides emergency relief for damaged communities in 25 countries. To improve quality of life for these communities, it does everything from caring for war-traumatized children to providing health care and building schools.

Break it down!

Ninety cents out of every dollar go straight to the programs. The rest goes to management and fund-raising.

Anything else I should know?

International Rescue Committee began as a European organization. An American branch was founded when Albert Einstein suggested that they do so to help Germans suffering under Hitler.

How can I donate or get more information on this charity?

Internet: www.theirc.org
Email: irc@theirc.org
Phone: (212) 551-3000
Fax: (212) 551-3180
Mail: 122 East 42nd Street, New York, NY 10168

Lance Armstrong Foundation

What is the organization's mission?

To improve the quality of life of people living with cancer. It provides practical information and tools to inspire and empower them to "live strong."

How will the organization spend my money?

The foundation spends money for community programs, public education, advocacy efforts, and cancer research.

Break it down!

Just over 85 cents of every dollar go to support the cause. The rest is for management and fund-raising expenses.

Anything else I should know?

The foundation was founded in 1997 by champion bicyclist Lance Armstrong, who survived cancer. One in three Americans will get cancer in their lifetimes.

How can I donate or get more information on this charity?

Internet: www.livestrong.org
Email: donations@laf.org
Phone: (512) 236-8820 to make a donation or for general information; (866) 235-7205 for support services for people affected by cancer
Fax: none
Mail: P.O. Box 161150, Austin, TX 78716-1150

Make-A-Wish Foundation International

What is the organization's mission?

To give children with life-threatening illnesses hope, strength, and joy by granting their wishes.

How will the organization spend my money?

Donations are used to help ill children go to places they've always dreamed of going, meet their heroes, become things they wish to be, learn to do things that excite them, and have things they yearn for.

Break it down!

More than 82 percent of total revenue is dedicated to wish-granting efforts. The rest goes towards management and overhead fees.

Anything else I should know?

The Make-A-Wish Foundation was founded in 1980 by a boy named Chris Greicius, who was granted his wish of becoming a police officer. Since then, the organization has granted more than 144,000 wishes to kids around the world.

How can I donate or get more information on this charity?

Internet: www.worldwish.org
Email: through web site
Phone: (602) 230-9900; (800) 965-9474
Fax: (602) 230-9627
Mail: 4041 North Central Avenue, Suite 555, Phoenix, AR 85012

March of Dimes

What is the organization's mission?
To improve the health of babies by preventing birth defects, premature birth, and infant mortality.

How will the organization spend my money?
The March of Dimes carries out its mission through research, community services, education, and advocacy to save babies' lives.

Break it down!
Seventy-five cents of every dollar go to the programs, seven cents to management, and 18 cents to fund-raising.

Anything else I should know?
President Franklin D. Roosevelt, who used a wheelchair as a result of his battle with polio, founded the March of Dimes in 1938.

How can I donate or get more information on this charity?
Internet: www.marchofdimes.com
Email: askus@marchofdimes.com
Phone: (800) 658-6674
Fax: (914) 997-4537
En Español Phone: 800-925-1855
Internet: www.nacersano.org
Mail: 1275 Mamaroneck Avenue, White Plains, NY 10605

Meals on Wheels

What is the organization's mission?

To support vulnerable Americans by providing social, physical, nutritional, and economic help.

How will the organization spend my money?

The Meals on Wheels Association of America helps local Meals on Wheels organizations around the country. The local groups conduct nutrition programs and deliver food to people who are unable to shop or prepare food for themselves, because they are elderly, frail, or disabled.

Break it down!

Eighty-four cents of every dollar go to program expenses, while 11 cents go to administration and five cents to fund-raising.

Anything else I should know?

Originally a British group, the American Meals on Wheels program started in Philadelphia in 1954. Most of the original volunteers were high school students. They delivered plates of food door-to-door and were nicknamed "Platter Angels."

How can I donate or get more information on this charity?

Internet: www.mowaa.org
Email: mowaa@mowaa.org
Phone: (703) 548-5558
Fax: (703) 548-8024
Mail: 203 S. Union Street, Alexandria, VA 22314

National Center for Missing & Exploited Children (NCMEC)

What is the organization's mission?

To help prevent child abduction and sexual exploitation; help find missing children; and assist victims of child abduction and sexual exploitation, their families, and the professionals who serve them.

How will the organization spend my money?

NCMEC will spend the money on programs and services directed at locating and recovering missing children and preventing the victimization of children.

Break it down!

Ninety-four cents of every dollar go directly to support programs.

Anything else I should know?

Since its establishment in 1984, NCMEC has assisted law enforcement with more than 111,000 missing child cases, resulting in the recovery of more than 96,900 children.

How can I donate or get more information on this charity?

Internet: www.missingkids.com
Phone: (703) 274-3900 for information;
(800) THE-LOST for the 24-hour hotline
Fax: (703) 274-2200
Mail: Charles B. Wang International Children's Building,
699 Prince Street, Alexandria, VA 22314

Orphan Foundation of America (OFA)

What is the organization's mission?

To help older kids who live in foster care by providing scholarships, mentoring support, and training in independent living skills, so that they can become productive, self-reliant adults.

How will the organization spend my money?

OFA promotes national awareness about America's foster youth, provides education for orphans through a scholarship program, and offers opportunities for the public to help foster children in college.

Break it down!

About 98 cents of every dollar go toward helping parentless children and teens. The other two cents go towards administration and fund-raising.

Anything else I should know?

OFA has given almost $11 million to thousands of students across the country through their scholarship program.

How can I donate or get more information on this charity?

Internet: www.orphan.org
Email: help@orphan.org
Phone: (571) 203-0270
Fax: (571) 203-0273
Mail: 21351 Gentry Drive, Suite 130, Sterling, VA 20166

Project HOPE (Health Opportunities for People Everywhere)

What is the organization's mission?

To provide health care and health education to those in need worldwide.

How will the organization spend my money?

Donations are used to fight infectious diseases (such as AIDS and tuberculosis); to train health workers; to help create and manage Village Health Banks that provide health education and offer loans; to improve hospitals; and to educate people about important health issues.

Break it down!

About 93 cents of every dollar go straight to the programs. The other seven cents is used for managing the organization.

Anything else I should know?

Project HOPE now provides more than $100 million worth of resources on five continents each year.

How can I donate or get more information on this charity?

Internet: www.projecthope.org
Email: webmaster@projecthope.org
Phone: (540) 837-2100; (800) 544-4673
Fax: (540) 837-1813
Mail: 255 Carter Hall Lane, Millwood, VA 22646

Save the Children

What is the organization's mission?

To improve the lives of families in need, through immediate aid as well as long-term assistance.

How will the organization spend my money?

Donations help children by battling hunger and poverty, and by supporting and offering health care, education, economic opportunities, and emergency assistance.

Break it down!

About 90 cents per dollar is spent delivering program services. About six cents is for fund-raising and four cents for management.

Anything else I should know?

One in six kids in the United States lives in poverty!

How can I donate or get more information on this charity?

Internet: www.savethechildren.org
Email: twebster@savechildren.org
Phone: (800) 728-3843
Fax: (203) 221-4205
Mail: 54 Wilton Road, Westport, CT 06880

SOS Children's Villages

What is the organization's mission?

To give long-term family-based care and stable environments to children who have lost their parents or who are unable to live with their parents because of war, natural disasters, or other long-term problems.

How will the organization spend my money?

Donations are used to create family houses where four to ten boys and girls live like brothers and sisters with an "SOS mother." Eight to fifteen houses join together as a village community.

Break it down!

More than 90% of sponsorship donations go directly to the children or villages. Other non-sponsorship donations provide support for SOS facilities' construction and operating costs, and for administrative purposes.

Anything else I should know?

SOS runs 449 children's villages, 335 youth facilities, 260 kindergartens, 173 primary schools, 115 vocational schools, 258 social centers, 53 medical centers, and 9 emergency aid programs in 132 countries and territories.

How can I donate or get more information on this charity?

Internet: www.sos-childrensvillages.org
Email: info@sos-childrensvillages.org
Phone: 43 (1) 368 66 78
Fax: 43 (1) 369 89 18
Mail: Billrothstr. 22, A-1190 Vienna, Austria

Stand for Children

What is the organization's mission?

To make sure that all children in America have an opportunity to grow up healthy, educated, and safe.

How will the organization spend my money?

Stand for Children spends money pushing the government to pass laws and develop programs that help children on a local, state, and national level. So far, its work has resulted in over $509,325,485 being spent on schools, after-school programs, free lunches, the adding of fluoride to water, and more.

Break it down!

Almost 85 cents of every dollar go straight to the programs. Eight cents go toward covering management and seven cents toward fund-raising.

Anything else I should know?

June 1 is Stand for Children Day in honor of a historic rally for children that happened on June 1, 1996, in Washington, D.C. It was the largest rally for children in the history of the United States.

How can I donate or get more information on this charity?

Internet: www.stand.org
Email: stand@stand.org
Phone: (800) 663-4032
Fax: (503) 963-9517
Mail: 516 SE Morrison Street, Suite 420, Portland, OR 97214

The Susan G. Komen Breast Cancer Foundation

What is the organization's mission?

To eradicate breast cancer as a life-threatening disease by advancing research, education, screening, and treatment.

How will the organization spend my money?

A global leader in the fight against breast cancer, the Komen Foundation fulfills its mission through support of innovative breast cancer research grants; meritorious awards; and educational, scientific, and community outreach programs around the world.

Break it down!

Eighty-one cents of every dollar fund mission programs.

Anything else I should know?

Every year more than 1 million people participate in the Komen Race for the Cure, a series of 5-K runs that raise both money and awareness for the fight against breast cancer.

How can I donate or get more information on this charity?

Internet: www.komen.org
Email: helpline@komen.org
Phone: (800) 462-9273; 1 (800) I'M AWARE
Fax: (972) 855-1605
Mail: P.O. Box 650309, Dallas, TX 75265

UNICEF, the United Nations Children's Fund

What is the organization's mission?

To protect and defend children's rights, to help meet children's basic needs, and to expand opportunities for children to reach their full potential.

How will the organization spend my money?

On improving the lives of disadvantaged children through programs that deal with war, disasters, extreme poverty, health care (immunization and HIV/AIDS), education, equality, and protection from violence and exploitation.

Break it down!

Eighty-seven cents of every dollar go directly towards programs.

Anything else I should know?

Every year, more than 10 million children die totally preventable deaths. Six million of these lives could be saved by basic, cost-saving measures . . . such as vaccines, antibiotics, micronutrient supplementation, insecticide-treated bed nets, and improved breast-feeding practices.

How can I donate or get more information on this charity?

Internet: www.unicef.org
Email: information@unicefusa.org
Phone: (212) 686-5522 for information;
(800) 4-UNICEF to make a donation
Fax: (212) 779-1679
Mail: 3 United Nations Plaza, New York, NY 10017 for information;
333 E. 38th Street, New York, NY 10016 to make a donation

United Negro College Fund

What is the organization's mission?

To provide financial assistance to deserving students, raise operating funds for member schools, and increase access to technology for students and faculty at historically black colleges and universities.

How will the organization spend my money?

To provide operating funds and technology enhancement services for 39 member historically black colleges and universities; scholarships and internships for students at about 900 institutions; and faculty and administrative professional training.

Break it down!

81 cents out of every dollar go toward the programs. Nine cents go to running the organization and 10 cents go to fund-raising.

Anything else I should know?

The United Negro College Fund has raised more than $2 billion to help more than 350,000 students attend college, and has distributed more funds to help minorities attend school than any entity outside of the government.

How can I donate or get more information on this charity?

Internet: www.uncf.org
Email: through web site
Phone: (800) 331-2244
Fax: none
Mail: 8260 Willow Oaks Corporate Drive, P.O. Box 10444, Fairfax, VA 22031

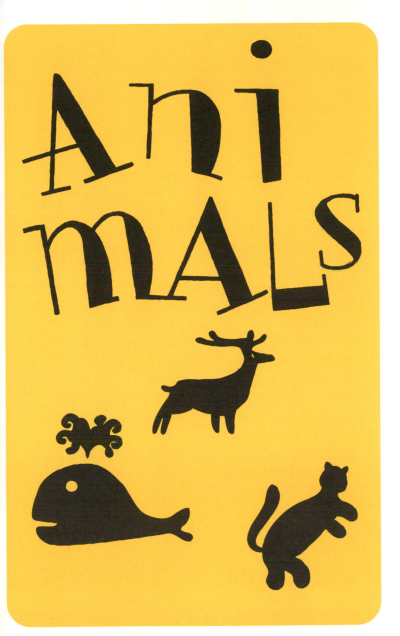

African Wildlife Foundation
Alley Cat Allies
American Eagle Foundation
American Society for the
  Prevention of Cruelty to Animals
Animal Protection Institute
Animal Welfare Institute
Bat Conservation International
Big Cat Rescue
Chimp Haven
Days End Farm Horse Rescue
Defenders of Wildlife
The Delta Society
The Elephant Sanctuary
Farm Animal Reform Movement
Fund for Animals
Greyhound Pets of America
HawkWatch International
Humane Farming Association
In Defense of Animals
International Fund for Animal
  Welfare
The Jane Goodall Institute

Last Chance for Animals
The Marine Mammal Center
National Wildlife Federation
Native American Fish
  and Wildlife Society
Paws With A Cause
People for the Ethical Treatment
  of Animals
The Peregrine Fund
The Rocky Mountain Elk Foundation
United Animal Nations
WildCare
Wildlife Conservation Society
World Society for the Protection
  of Animals
World Wildlife Fund

African Wildlife Foundation (AWF)

What is the organization's mission?

To work together with the people of Africa to ensure the wildlife and wild lands of Africa will endure forever.

How will the organization spend my money?

It works across Africa helping to establish wildlife protection areas, known as Heartlands, which are vital to the preservation of elephants, mountain gorillas, cheetahs, rhinos, and other wildlife. AWF also supports scientific research that addresses the conservation of Africa's wildlife treasures.

Break it down!

Around 87 cents of every dollar donated go to helping the animals. The rest is put aside for fund-raising and for management.

Anything else I should know?

AWF helps wildlife and people. It improves people's lives by helping start eco-businesses and by providing leadership training. It supports research and protection of endangered species and conserves large, healthy landscapes.

How can I donate or get more information on this charity?

Internet: www.awf.org
Email: africanwildlife@awf.org
Phone: (202) 939-3333 or (888) 494-5354
Fax: (202) 939-3332
Mail: 1400 16th Street, NW, Suite 120, Washington, DC 20036

Alley Cat Allies

What is the organization's mission?

To promote and advocate Trap-Neuter-Return and other nonlethal methods to control and reduce outdoor cat populations.

How will the organization spend my money?

Alley Cat Allies educates the public and municipalities about feline overpopulation and ways to solve the problem without cruelty. It also trains caregivers and works to change local animal control laws, so even more cats can live out their natural lives in managed colonies without being killed in shelters.

Break it down!

Seventy-eight cents of each dollar are used for program expenses. About 16 cents go to fund-raising and development and six cents to administrative costs.

Anything else I should know?

National Feral Cat Day (October 16) was created by Alley Cat Allies in 2001. A feral cat is one who has "gone wild" and can no longer be adopted into homes. Feral Cat Day is a day where people educate their communities about safe and friendly feral cat and kitten population control.

How can I donate or get more information on this charity?

Internet: www.alleycat.org
Email: alleycat@alleycat.org
Phone: (240) 482-1980
Fax: (240) 482-1990
Mail: 7920 Norfolk Avenue, Suite 600, Bethesda, MD 20814

American Eagle Foundation

What is the organization's mission?
To protect the bald eagle (the national symbol of the United States of America) and its habitat.

How will the organization spend my money?
It supports and conducts eagle recovery programs, environmental recovery programs, and educational programs. It not only tries to protect eagles in our environment and ecosystem, but also cares for injured and orphaned eagles at its Pigeon Forge, Tennessee, eagle center.

Break it down!
Eighty-three cents of every dollar go towards the programs, 13 cents to management, and four cents to fund-raising.

Anything else I should know?
The American Eagle Foundation runs the largest bald eagle breeding facilities in the world and has an eagle adoption program.

How can I donate or get more information on this charity?
Internet: www.eagles.org
Email: EagleMail@Eagles.Org
Phone: (800) 2EAGLES
Fax: (865) 429-4743
Mail: P.O. Box 333, Pigeon Forge, TN 37868

American Society for the Prevention of Cruelty to Animals (ASPCA)

What is the organization's mission?
To alleviate pain, fear, and suffering in all animals.

How will the organization spend my money?
The ASPCA helps animals directly at its New York City headquarters through adoptions, veterinary care, and humane law enforcement. Across the country, the ASPCA provides educational and shelter outreach programs, lobbies for animal legislation, and advocates on behalf of all animals.

Break it down!
Approximately 78 cents of every dollar go to programs that fight animal cruelty. About one cent goes to administration and 21 cents is spent on fund-raising.

Anything else I should know?
The ASPCA is the oldest humane organization in America and was founded in 1866 by Henry Bergh, a philanthropist and diplomat who recognized that many animals suffer from inhumane treatment in our society.

How can I donate or get more information on this charity?
Internet: www.aspca.org
Email: through web site
Phone: (212) 876-7700
Fax: (212) 423-9813
Mail: 424 East 92nd Street, New York, NY 10128

Animal Protection Institute (API)

What is the organization's mission?

To end animal abuse and exploitation.

How will the organization spend my money?

With a focus on animals used in entertainment, exotic "pets," animals used in research and product testing, wildlife, companion animals, and farm animals, API protects animals through the use of legislation, litigation, advocacy, and public education. API works at all levels: local, state, national, and international.

Break it down!

Approximately 79 cents of each dollar go toward animal protection. Thirteen cents go to management and eight to fund-raising.

Anything else I should know?

API operates a sanctuary in Dilley, Texas, that provides a free-ranging environment to more than 400 nonhuman primates.

How can I donate or get more information on this charity?

Internet: www.api4animals.org
Email: info@api4animals.org
Phone: (916) 447-3085
Fax: (916) 447-3070
Mail: P.O. Box 22505, Sacramento, CA 95822

Animal Welfare Institute (AWI)

What is the organization's mission?

To reduce the pain and fear that humans inflict on animals.

How will the organization spend my money?

Donations are used to fight for humane treatment of labora-
tory animals; to develop non-animal testing; to preserve
endangered species; to stop cruelty to farm animals who are
raised in "animal factories"; and to make people aware of
animal welfare issues.

Break it down!

Eighty-five cents of every dollar go toward the programs. Roughly
two cents go to fund-raising and 13 to overhead.

Anything else I should know?

Founded in 1951, AWI publishes a magazine, the *AWI
Quarterly*, which keeps you posted on their progress.

How can I donate or get more information on this charity?

Internet: www.awionline.org
Email: awi@awionline.org
Phone: (703) 836-4300
Fax: (703) 836-0400
Mail: P.O. Box 3650, Washington, DC 20027

Bat Conservation International

What is the organization's mission?

To protect bats, restore their habitats around the world, and educate the public about them.

How will the organization spend my money?

Its programs teach people to understand and value bats as essential allies; protect critical bat habitats and encourage others to join in conservation efforts; and use research to advance scientific knowledge about bats, their conservation needs, and the ecosystems that rely on them.

Break it down!

About 80 cents of each dollar go to the programs, 11 cents to fund-raising, and nine cents to administration.

Anything else I should know?

Bat Conservation International has an adopt-a-bat program. For a one-time contribution of $15, you get a photo of your bat, an adoption certificate, species information, a letter from your bat, and a bat bumper sticker.

How can I donate or get more information on this charity?

Internet: www.batcon.org
Email: batinfo@batcon.org
Phone: (512) 327-9721
Fax: (512) 327-9724
Mail: P.O. Box 162603, Austin, TX 78716

Big Cat Rescue

What is the organization's mission?
To end the suffering of wild cats.

How will the organization spend my money?
They rescue big cats and rehabilitate them in an educational center that is open to the public, with hopes of someday re-releasing the cats into their native environment.

Break it down!
About 63 cents go directly to the animal care. The remainder is divided between fund-raising and management costs.

Anything else I should know?
In Big Cat Rescue's Adopt-a-Cat donation program, a donation of $25 lets you choose a number of different cats to sponsor.

How can I donate or get more information on this charity?
Internet: www.bigcatrescue.org
Email: Info@BigCatRescue.org
Phone: (813) 920-4130
Fax: (813) 920-5924
Mail: 12802 Easy Street, Tampa, FL 33625

Chimp Haven

What is the organization's mission?

To care for chimpanzees who were previously used for medical research, as pets, or in entertainment.

How will the organization spend my money?

Donations go towards the chimpanzees' care and the construction of suitable forest habitats where they can live out the rest of their lives in social groups.

Break it down!

Chimp Haven has finished its first multi-acre habitat, and the first chimpanzees arrived in April 2005. $2.5 million is necessary to complete construction of the sanctuary's second phase in time to accommodate Chimp Haven's coming residents.

Anything else I should know?

Chimp Haven was selected by the United States government to be the National Chimpanzee Sanctuary. Located in northwest Louisiana, the sanctuary occupies 200 acres of lush, forested land. Upon completion of all three phases of the sanctuary, Chimp Haven plans to care for up to 300 chimpanzees.

How can I donate or get more information on this charity?

Internet: www.chimphaven.org
Email: information@chimphaven.org
Phone: (888) 98-CHIMP (24467)
Fax: (318) 925-6024
Mail: 13600 Chimpanzee Place, Keithville, LA 71047

Days End Farm Horse Rescue

What is the organization's mission?

To foster compassion and responsibility for horses through intervention, education, and outreach.

How will the organization spend my money?

Donations are used for program services; educational programs; rescue and rehabilitation of abused or neglected horses; disaster services and emergency rescue; and outreach programs.

Break it down!

Eighty-four cents of every dollar received go to program services. Eight cents go to management and general costs, and eight cents go to fund-raising.

Anything else I should know?

The facilities house around 50 to 60 horses at any given time. Over 500 kids and adults work as volunteers; kids under 12 must have a parent or guardian working along with them.

How can I donate or get more information on this charity?

Internet: www.defhr.org
Email: defhr@erols.com
Phone: (301) 854-5037; (401) 442-1564
Fax: (301) 854-5146
Mail: 15856 Frederick Road, Lisbon, MD 21765

Defenders of Wildlife

What is the organization's mission?

To protect all native wild animals and plants in their natural communities.

How will the organization spend my money?

Defenders of Wildlife targets what it considers to be the biggest threats to the environment: "the accelerating rate of extinction of species and the associated loss of biological diversity, and habitat alteration and destruction." They also fight to conserve entire ecosystems.

Break it down!

Seventy-five cents of every dollar go toward programs. Eleven cents go to management and 14 cents go to fund-raising.

Anything else I should know?

They have a wildlife adoption program, where you can sponsor a specific species, such as a wolf, elephant, sea otter, or other endangered animal.

How can I donate or get more information on this charity?

Internet: www.defenders.org
Email: defenders@mail.defenders.org
Phone: (800) 989-8981
Fax: none
Mail: 1130 17th Street, NW, Washington, DC 20036

The Delta Society

What is the organization's mission?

To promote mutually beneficial relationships with animals to improve people's health, independence, and quality of life.

How will the organization spend my money?

The Delta Society uses donations to help people through animal-assisted activities and therapy, providing advocacy for people with disabilities who have service dogs, creating a curriculum for trainers of service dogs, and providing information about the health benefits of contact with animals.

Break it down!

About 63 cents of every dollar go directly to the programs. About seven cents go to management and 30 cents go to fund-raising.

Anything else I should know?

The Delta Society runs many different programs that help bring people and animals together, such as animal-assisted therapy, providing pets to people with special needs, dog training, and more.

How can I donate or get more information on this charity?

Internet: www.deltasociety.org
Email: info@deltasociety.org
Phone: (425) 226-7357
Fax: (425) 235-1076
Mail: 875 124th Ave, NE, Suite 101, Bellevue, WA 98005

The Elephant Sanctuary

What is the organization's mission?

To provide sick, needy, and elderly elephants with a home, and to educate the public about endangered elephants.

How will the organization spend my money?

Donations are used to expand and maintain The Elephant Sanctuary, to care for the elephants by providing them with things like food and medicine, and to educate the public.

Break it down!

Eighty-six cents of every dollar go straight to helping out the elephants, while five cents go to administration and nine cents to fund-raising.

Anything else I should know?

The sanctuary currently houses three African and eleven Asian elephants. You can see pictures and video of them through the "Elecam" located on the organization's web site.

How can I donate or get more information on this charity?

Internet: www.elephants.com
Email: elephant@elephants.com
Phone: (931) 796-6500
Fax: (931) 796-4810
Mail: P.O. Box 393, Hohenwald, TN 38462

Farm Animal Reform Movement (FARM)

What is the organization's mission?

To advocate a "plant-based diet and humane treatment of farmed animals."

How will the organization spend my money?

Farm Animal Reform Movement uses contributions toward campaigns such as The Great American Meatout and World Farm Animals Day for which FARM coordinates educational events in thousands of communities across the country.

Break it down!

FARM has an overhead of less than five cents of every dollar and spends very little on fund-raising, so contributions go directly to support the programs.

Anything else I should know?

Over 30 million Americans have explored a vegetarian diet.

How can I donate or get more information on this charity?

Internet: www.farmusa.org
Email: info@farmusa.org
Phone: (888) ASK-FARM
Fax: none
Mail: 10101 Ashburton Lane, Bethesda, MD 20817

Fund for Animals

What is the organization's mission?

To protect animals and maintain that there are humane ways to deal with human/animal conflicts with no rationalization for cruelty.

How will the organization spend my money?

The Fund for Animals employs four tactics in its efforts to protect animals from cruelty: education, legislation, litigation, and hands-on care.

Break it down!

Seventy-nine cents of every dollar go towards the fund's programs. Ten cents go to fund-raising and eleven cents go to management.

Anything else I should know?

With regional offices working around the country on animal campaigns and animal care facilities, such as the world-famous Black Beauty Ranch, the fund is one of the largest and most active organizations working for the cause of animals throughout the world.

How can I donate or get more information on this charity?

Internet: www.fundforanimals.org
Email: fundinfo@fund.org
Phone: (888) 405-FUND
Fax: (212) 246-2633
Mail: 200 West 57th Street, New York, NY 10019

Greyhound Pets of America

What is the organization's mission?

To find good homes for greyhounds who were used for dog racing and to educate the public about these wonderful dogs.

How will the organization spend my money?

Donations are used to locate homes for the dogs and to care for the dogs before they are adopted.

Break it down!

Ninety-five cents of every dollar go toward the programs. About three cents go to running the organization and two cents go to fund-raising.

Anything else I should know?

Since 1987, they have found homes for over 65,000 greyhounds!

How can I donate or get more information on this charity?

Internet: www.greyhoundpets.org
Email: greyhoundpets@greyhoundpets.org
Phone: (800) 366-1472
Fax: none
Mail: 6315 Greenvale Lane, Houston, TX 77066

HawkWatch International

What is the organization's mission?

To protect hawks, eagles, other birds of prey, and our environment through research, conservation, and education.

How will the organization spend my money?

Your money goes towards things like funding raptor research stations and education programs that help promote environmental awareness.

Break it down!

Eighty-eight cents of each dollar go directly to HawkWatch. The remaining twelve cents is for overhead and fund-raising.

Anything else I should know?

Because they are at the top of the food chain, raptors (birds of prey) are good indicators of whether an ecosystem is healthy or not. People share these ecosystems with raptors—and whatever happens to them will happen to us.

How can I donate or get more information on this charity?

Internet: www.hawkwatch.org
Email: hwi@hawkwatch.org
Phone: (801) 484-6808
Fax: (801) 484-6810
Mail: 1800 South West Temple, Ste. 226, Salt Lake City, UT 84115

Humane Farming Association

What is the organization's mission?

To protect farm animals from cruelty; to protect people from antibiotics, hormones, and other chemicals misused on factory farms; and to protect the environment from the impact of large-scale industrial farming factories.

How will the organization spend my money?

Donations are used for programs that expose animal cruelty, educate the public, offer emergency care for animals that need help, and more.

Break it down!

About 91 cents of every dollar go toward program services. A little over three cents go to management and six cents go to fund-raising.

Anything else I should know?

The Humane Farming Association was founded in 1985 and now has over 185,000 members and volunteers.

How can I donate or get more information on this charity?

Internet: www.hfa.org
Email: hfa@hfa.org
Phone: (415) 771-CALF
Fax: (415) 485-0106
Mail: P.O. Box 3577, San Rafael, CA 94912

In Defense of Animals

What is the organization's mission?

To raise the status of animals above that of mere property; to end the exploitation and abuse of animals; and to defend their rights, welfare, and habitat.

How will the organization spend my money?

Donations are used to support education campaigns, animal abuse investigations, and animal rescue and rehabilitation in In Defense of Animals facilities in Mississippi and Africa.

Break it down!

Eighty-four cents of every dollar go to program services. Five cents are for management and 11 cents go to fund-raising.

Anything else I should know?

In Defense of Animals has an amazing history of accomplishments, which include creating a chimpanzee sanctuary in Cameroon, Africa, for orphaned and abused chimps.

How can I donate or get more information on this charity?

Internet: www.idausa.org
Email: ida@idausa.org
Phone: (415) 388-9641
Fax: (415) 388-0388
Mail: 131 Camino Alto, Mill Valley, CA 94941

International Fund for Animal Welfare

What is the organization's mission?

To improve the welfare of wild and domestic animals throughout the world by reducing commercial exploitation of animals, protecting wildlife habitats, and assisting animals in distress.

How will the organization spend my money?

The International Fund for Animal Welfare engages communities, government leaders, and like-minded organizations around the world to achieve lasting solutions to pressing animal welfare and conservation challenges.

Break it down!

Seventy-three cents of every dollar go directly to animal welfare programs. About 11 cents go to management costs and 16 cents to fund-raising.

Anything else I should know?

The fund works to save animals at risk like seals, dolphins, porpoises, whales, bears, elephants, rhinos, primates, and pets.

How can I donate or get more information on this charity?

Internet: www.ifaw.org
Email: info@ifaw.org
Phone: (508) 744-2000
Fax: (508) 744-2009
Mail: 411 Main Street, Yarmouth Port, MA 02675

The Jane Goodall Institute

What is the organization's mission?

To increase public awareness, expand primate habitat conservation, conduct behavioral research of chimpanzees in the wild, and protect chimps and other primates. The organization also partners with local communities in Africa to help improve lives through health care, education, improved agriculture, and other means.

How will the organization spend my money?

Donations are spent to run safe, loving sanctuaries for orphan chimpanzees; to educate people about the importance of conservation; to continue Dr. Goodall's chimpanzee research in Tanzania; to support Roots & Shoots, the institute's global youth program that assists young people as they take action in their communities and beyond; and to run community-centered conservation programs in Africa.

Break it down!

Out of every dollar, 68 cents go to the programs, 16 cents go to fundraising, and 16 cents go to management.

Anything else I should know?

Jane Goodall was just 26 years old when she went to Tanzania to live with and study chimpanzees in 1960.

How can I donate or get more information on this charity?

Internet: www.janegoodall.org
Email: info@janegoodall.org
Phone: (703) 682-9220, and ask for development (re: donations) or for Roots & Shoots (re: educational programs)
Fax: (703) 682-9312
Mail: 4245 North Fairfax Drive, Suite 600, Arlington, VA 22203

Last Chance for Animals (LCA)

What is the organization's mission?

To recognize that animals have the ability to experience pain and that they deserve certain basic rights protecting them from pain caused by humans.

How will the organization spend my money?

Last Chance for Animals uses peaceful action to investigate and expose forms of animal injustice and cruelty. It also has campaigns to educate and inform the public.

Break it down!

Approximately 79 cents go directly to the organization's campaigns. About two cents go to management expenses and 19 go to fund-raising.

Anything else I should know?

LCA believes that humans should not subject animals to suffering and exploitation because alternatives exist for nearly every traditional "usage" of animals. It therefore opposes the use of animals for food, entertainment, clothing, and scientific experimentation.

How can I donate or get more information on this charity?

Internet: www.lcanimal.org
Email: through web site
Phone: (310) 271-6096
Fax: (310) 271-1890
Mail: 8033 Sunset Blvd, #835, Los Angeles, CA 90046

The Marine Mammal Center

What is the organization's mission?

To ensure the survival and conservation of marine mammals and their habitat.

How will the organization spend my money?

Donations are spent on rescue, rehabilitation, and scientific research; they are also used to educate the public about the marine environment and its importance to all forms of life.

Break it down!

Seventy-two cents of every dollar donated go directly to fund programs. Nineteen cents go toward fund-raising and nine cents go to support services.

Anything else I should know?

Since 1975, more than 11,500 marine mammals—including sea otters, dolphins, sea lions, and many types of seals—have been treated at the center's hospital facility.

How can I donate or get more information on this charity?

Internet: www.marinemammalcenter.org
Email: through web site
Phone: (415) 289-SEAL
Fax: (415) 289-7333
Mail: Marin Headlands, 1065 Fort Cronkhite, Sausalito, CA 94965

National Wildlife Federation

What is the organization's mission?

To educate, inspire, and assist individuals and organizations of diverse cultures to conserve wildlife and other natural resources and to protect the Earth's environment in order to achieve a peaceful, equitable, and sustainable future.

How will the organization spend my money?

The National Wildlife Federation launches conservation programs all over the country and has outreach programs to educate the public.

Break it down!

Around 82 cents of every dollar go to conservation and education programs. The rest of the money is for supporting services.

Anything else I should know?

Founded in 1936, it is one of the nation's largest and oldest protectors of wildlife. With more than four million members and supporters, it is committed to educating and empowering people from all walks of life to protect wildlife and habitat for future generations.

How can I donate or get more information on this charity?

Internet: www.nwf.org
Email: through web site
Phone: (800) 822-9919
Fax: none
Mail: 11100 Wildlife Center Drive, Reston, VA 20190

Native American Fish and Wildlife Society

What is the organization's mission?

To protect, preserve, and enhance Native American fish and wildlife resources.

How will the organization spend my money?

Donations go to educate Native Americans involved in fish and wildlife management and to improve the general welfare of tribal people through educational, charitable, as well as fish and wildlife enhancement activities.

Break it down!

About 80 cents of every dollar go to program services. The other 20 cents are for management and general costs.

Anything else I should know?

The society represents professional biologists, natural resource managers, technicians, and conservation law enforcement officers.

How can I donate or get more information on this charity?

Internet: www.nafws.org
Email: webmaster@nafws.org
Phone: (303) 466-1725
Fax: (303) 466-5414
Mail: 8333 Greenwood Blvd., Suite 250, Denver, CO 80221

Paws With A Cause

What is the organization's mission?

To encourage independence for people with disabilities around the country by training assistance dogs, providing lifetime team support, and educating the general public about the importance of assistance dogs.

How will the organization spend my money?

Due to a lack of trainable dogs in humane societies and animal shelters across the country, PAWS now has a breeding program to produce future assistance dogs. Once they are trained, they are placed into homes, where they go to work helping people.

Break it down!

Approximately 95 cents of every donated dollar go to programs. Three cents is for fund-raising and two cents go to running the office.

Anything else I should know?

Only 3% of people with disabilities are blind; the other 97% are physically challenged in some other way. Other than Paws With A Cause, there are very few organizations training dogs to work with disabled people who are not blind.

How can I donate or get more information on this charity?

Internet: www.pawswithacause.org
Email: paws@pawswithacause.org
Phone: (800) 253-PAWS
Fax: (616) 877-0248
Mail: National Headquarters, 4646 South Division, Wayland, MI 49348

People for the Ethical Treatment of Animals (PETA)

What is the organization's mission?

To establish and protect the rights of all animals and to operate under the simple principle that animals are not ours to eat, wear, experiment on, or use for entertainment.

How will the organization spend my money?

Founded in 1980, PETA focuses on four areas of animal cruelty: factory farms, laboratories, the fur trade, and the entertainment industry. It fights for its cause through "public education, cruelty investigations, research, animal rescue, legislation, special events, celebrity involvement, and protest campaigns."

Break it down!

About 86 cents of every dollar go to program support, while three cents go to management and general operations, and 11 cents go to fund-raising.

Anything else I should know?

People for the Ethical Treatment of Animals is the largest animal rights organization in the world.

How can I donate or get more information on this charity?

Internet: www.peta.org
Email: info@peta.org
Phone: (757) 622-PETA
Fax: (757) 622-0457
Mail: 501 Front Street, Norfolk, VA 23510

The Peregrine Fund

What is the organization's mission?

To conserve hawks, eagles, falcons, and other birds of prey in the wild.

How will the organization spend my money?

Donations are used to save species that are in jeopardy, to conserve habitats for birds of prey, to educate students and the public, and to train conservationists.

Break it down!

100% of every dollar goes directly to birds of prey projects.

There is an endowment that has a payout covering all management and fund-raising costs.

Anything else I should know?

Birds of prey are an important part of the world's biological system. Because they are at the top of the food chain, they are very sensitive to environmental changes, so it's important that their habitats are protected.

How can I donate or get more information on this charity?

Internet: www.peregrinefund.org
Email: tpf@peregrinefund.org
Phone: (208) 362-3716
Fax: (208) 362-2376
Mail: 5668 W. Flying Hawk Lane, Boise, ID 83709

The Rocky Mountain Elk Foundation

What is the organization's mission?

To ensure the future of elk, other wildlife, and their habitats.

How will the organization spend my money?

Donations are used to buy land where elks live and to protect elks that live on privately owned land; to increase the nutrition in the food that elks can forage; and to educate the public about conservation.

Break it down!

On average, 90 cents of every dollar go toward habitat conservation and education. Six cents go to administration costs and four to fund-raising.

Anything else I should know?

The foundation has protected and enhanced over 4.3 million acres of land for elks and other wildlife in North America since they began in 1984.

How can I donate or get more information on this charity?

Internet: www.elkfoundation.org
Email: info@rmef.org
Phone: (800) 225-5355
Fax: (406) 523-4550
Mail: 5705 Grant Creek Road, Missoula, MT 59808

United Animal Nations

What is the organization's mission?

To protect animals in danger or in need and to focus global attention on their plight.

How will the organization spend my money?

Donations are used to protect and rescue animals; to send Emergency Animal Rescue Service teams to areas affected by disasters; to publicize animal-related issues; to educate the public; to investigate animal abuse; to protect animal habitats; and more.

Break it down!

About 81 cents of each dollar go directly to programs. The rest goes to fund-raising and administration.

Anything else I should know?

United Animal Nations' small staff of nine can accomplish so much because of their dedicated corps of 2,500 volunteers nationwide.

How can I donate or get more information on this charity?

Internet: www.uan.org
Email: info@uan.org
Phone: (916) 429-2457
Fax: (916) 429-2456
Mail: P.O. Box 188890, Sacramento, CA 95818

WildCare

What is the organization's mission?

To inspire a vital connection among people, wildlife, and the natural world.

How will the organization spend my money?

Your donation will assist WildCare in educating people, especially children, about local wildlife and the importance of taking care of the environment for all living things. WildCare's rehabilitation hospital takes care of ill, injured, and orphaned wildlife so that they can be returned to the wild.

Break it down!

Approximately 65 cents of every dollar go to programs, while about nine cents go to management, and 26 cents go to fund-raising.

Anything else I should know?

Each year, WildCare treats over 4,000 animals at their wildlife hospital. WildCare also operates a 24-hour "Living With Wildlife" hotline and answers 12,000 questions a year about urban wildlife.

How can I donate or get more information on this charity?

Internet: www.wildcarebayarea.org
Email: info@wildcarebayarea.org
Phone: (415) 453-1000 for information;
(415) 456-SAVE for wildlife hotline
Fax: (415) 456-0594
Mail: 76 Albert Park Lane, San Rafael, CA 94901

Wildlife Conservation Society (WCS)

What is the organization's mission?

To save wildlife and wild lands throughout the world, including over 20 African countries, over 20 Asian countries, and the Amazon.

How will the organization spend my money?

Donations help WCS work with international governments to protect their countries' ecology, to create solutions that help both local people and local animals, and to support more field scientists than any other organization.

Break it down!

About 89 cents per dollar go directly to programs. Seven cents go to general management costs and four cents to fund-raising.

Anything else I should know?

WCS was founded in 1895. From its headquarters at the Bronx Zoo, it runs programs in 53 nations across Africa, Asia, Latin America and North America, protecting wild landscapes that are home to a vast variety of species from butterflies to tigers.

How can I donate or get more information on this charity?

Internet: www.wcs.org
Email: membership@wcs.org
Phone: (718) 220-5100
Fax: none
Mail: 2300 Southern Blvd, Bronx, NY 10460

World Society for the Protection of Animals

What is the organization's mission?

To raise the standard of animal welfare all around the world.

How will the organization spend my money?

Donations support campaigns against animal cruelty and abuse by creating and enforcing stronger protection laws. They also help animal rescue teams to protect animals in their natural environment and rescue animals from disasters.

Break it down!

Seventy-five cents of every dollar go to projects, education, campaigns, and public awareness. Five cents go to management and 20 cents go to fund-raising.

Anything else I should know?

This organization is the world's largest network of animal protection societies. It is the only animal protection organization to have consultative status at the United Nations and Council of Europe.

How can I donate or get more information on this charity?

Internet: www.wspa-americas.org
Email: wspa@wspausa.com
Phone: (508) 879-8350 or (800) 883-WSPA
Fax: (508) 620-0786
Mail: 34 Deloss Street, Framingham, MA 01702

World Wildlife Fund (WWF)

What is the organization's mission?

To protect the world's wildlife and wild lands.

How will the organization spend my money?

WWF uses donations to work on three global goals: protecting endangered species; saving endangered habitats; and addressing global threats, such as toxic pollution, over-fishing, and climate change.

Break it down!

About 80 cents per dollar go directly to funding the program, while six cents go to general administration, and 14 cents go to fund-raising.

Anything else I should know?

WWF has over five million members worldwide, making it the world's largest privately financed conservation organization.

How can I donate or get more information on this charity?

Internet: www.worldwildlife.org
Email: PIResponse@wwfus.org
Phone: (202) 293-4800
Fax: (202) 293-9211
Mail: 1250 Twenty-Fourth Street, NW, Washington, DC 20037

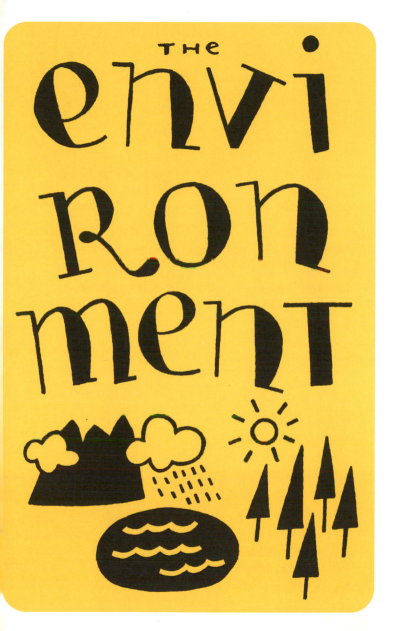

American Farmland Trust
American Forests
American Rivers
Beyond Pesticides
Center for Health, Environment and
	Justice
Clean Water Fund
Earthjustice
Environmental Defense
Friends of the Earth
Greenpeace
Inform, Inc.
Izaak Walton League of America
National Audubon Society
National Parks Conservation
	Association
National Resources Defense Council
The Nature Conservancy
The Ocean Conservancy
Pesticide Action Network
Rails-to-Trails Conservancy
Rainforest Action Network
Rainforest Alliance

The Rocky Mountain Institute
Scenic America
The Sierra Club Foundation
Student Conservation Association
The Surfrider Foundation
Trust for Public Land
The Wilderness Society

American Farmland Trust

What is the organization's mission?

To stop the disappearance of productive farmland in the United States and to promote farming methods that support a healthy environment.

How will the organization spend my money?

Donations are used to encourage conservation practices that keep the land healthy; to protect the best land through public programs; and to manage community growth in ways that support agriculture.

Break it down!

Seventy-six cents of each dollar go to program activities and 24 cents go to fund-raising and administration support.

Anything else I should know?

Every single minute, America loses two acres of farmland.

How can I donate or get more information on this charity?

Internet: www.farmland.org
Email: info@farmland.org
Phone: (202) 331-7300
Fax: (202) 659-8339
Mail: 1200 18th St, NW, Suite 800, Washington, DC 20036

American Forests

What is the organization's mission?

To promote "healthy forest ecosystems in every community."

How will the organization spend my money?

Donations are used to plant trees in areas around the world to help rebuild forests that have been destroyed by natural disasters and to restore forests where important wildlife habitat has been lost; for example, planting trees in Russia to provide habitat for the 350 endangered Siberian tigers that still live there.

Break it down!

Seventy-two cents of every dollar go toward its programs. Seven cents go to fund-raising and 21 cents go to administration.

Anything else I should know?

It is the nation's oldest non-profit citizens' conservation organization, founded in 1875. To celebrate its 125th anniversary, it set a goal of planting 20 million trees. It planted the 20 millionth tree in October 2002.

How can I donate or get more information on this charity?

Internet: www.americanforests.org
Email: info@amfor.org
Phone: (202) 737-1944
Fax: (202) 737-2457
Mail: P.O. Box 2000, Washington, DC 20013

American Rivers

What is the organization's mission?

To keep American rivers healthy and natural and to restore damaged rivers to a state of natural health; to protect and restore the wide variety of life sustained by rivers.

How will the organization spend my money?

Donations help protect and restore rivers where a large majority of the population's drinking water comes from.

Break it down!

Approximately 80 cents of every dollar go directly to conservation programs. Fifteen cents go to fund-raising and five cents go to management.

Anything else I should know?

Over the years, American Rivers has worked with over 500 other conservation groups to build a list of America's most endangered rivers, so those rivers receive the attention they need.

How can I donate or get more information on this charity?

Internet: www.americanrivers.org
Email: amrivers@americanrivers.org
Phone: (202) 347-7550
Fax: (202) 347-9240
Mail: 1101 14th Street, NW, Suite 1400, Washington, DC 20005

Beyond Pesticides

What is the organization's mission?

To ensure that people today and future generations have safe air, water, land, and food by promoting safe alternatives to hazardous pesticides.

How will the organization spend my money?

Donations are used to educate the public about the health and environmental dangers of pesticides and to advocate alternatives, so that we may protect our environment and ourselves.

Break it down!

Ninety-seven cents of every dollar go to the programs, while one cent goes for management, and two cents for fund-raising.

Anything else I should know?

The organization puts out a quarterly publication, "Pesticides and You", as well as two monthly newsletters, the "School Pesticide Monitor" and "Technical Report." The publications provide news and information about the dangers of pesticides and what can be done to curb their use. Beyond Pesticides also functions as a clearinghouse of information about pesticides, alternatives, and organizing.

How can I donate or get more information on this charity?

Internet: www.beyondpesticides.org
Email: info@beyondpesticides.org
Phone: (202) 543-5450
Fax: (202) 543-4791
Mail: 701 E Street, SE, #200, Washington, DC 20003

Center for Health, Environment and Justice

What is the organization's mission?

To protect the right of people to have a clean, healthy environment regardless of their race or whether they are rich or poor.

How will the organization spend my money?

Donations are used to work with community groups on environmental issues such as toxic waste, solid waste, air pollution, incinerators, medical waste, radioactive waste, pesticides, sewage, and industrial pollution.

Break it down!

Eighty-nine cents of each dollar go to the programs, three cents go to management, and eight cents go to fund-raising.

Anything else I should know?

The organization works hard to protect orphaned or abused children, who often are at risk of living in dangerous environmental conditions.

How can I donate or get more information on this charity?

Internet: www.chej.org
Email: chej@chej.org
Phone: (703) 237-2249
Fax: (703) 237-8389
Mail: P.O. Box 6806, Falls Church, VA 22040

Clean Water Fund (CWF)

What is the organization's mission?

To bring different communities together in the search for sensible solutions that will protect our water resources, so people can have clean drinking water in the future.

How will the organization spend my money?

CWF uses donations to help people campaign successfully for cleaner and safer water and air and to protect people from toxic pollution in our homes, neighborhoods, and workplaces.

Break it down!

About 78 cents of every dollar go towards programs and eight cents go towards fund-raising. The other 14 cents go towards administrative costs.

Anything else I should know?

CWF offers free training sessions on how people can protect their drinking water. The purpose of the trainings is to empower citizens, educate them on what could possibly contaminate their water and give them the skills to do something about it.

How can I donate or get more information on this charity?

Internet: www.cleanwaterfund.org
Email: cwf@cleanwater.org
Phone: (202) 895-0432
Fax: (202) 895-0438
Mail: 4455 Connecticut Ave., NW, Suite A300-16, Washington, DC 20008

Earthjustice

What is the organization's mission?

To protect the magnificent places, wildlife, and natural resources of our planet; to defend everyone's right to have a healthy environment.

How will the organization spend my money?

"Earthjustice works through the courts to safeguard public lands, national forests, parks, and wilderness areas; to reduce air and water pollution; to prevent toxic contamination; and to preserve endangered species and wildlife habitat."

Break it down!

Sixty-five cents of every dollar go to support legal work. Twenty-five cents of every dollar go toward fund-raising efforts and ten cents of every dollar go to administrative expenses.

Anything else I should know?

Earthjustice works to protect and enforce legislation such as the Clean Air Act and Endangered Species Act.

How can I donate or get more information on this charity?

Internet: www.earthjustice.org
Email: info@earthjustice.org
Phone: (510) 550-6700
Fax: (510) 550-6740
Mail: 426 17th Street, 6th Floor, Oakland, CA 94612

Environmental Defense

What is the organization's mission?

To protect the rights of all people (including future generations) to clean air and water, healthy food, and thriving ecosystems.

How will the organization spend my money?

Environmental Defense spends donations to create lasting solutions that protect the oceans, ecosystems, environmental health, climate, and air.

Break it down!

Eighty cents of each dollar go to program work. Five cents go to management and administration and 15 cents go to fund-raising.

Anything else I should know?

The staff of Environmental Defense includes more Ph.D. scientists and economists than any other similar organization. They are helping to come up with practical solutions to the world's problems.

How can I donate or get more information on this charity?

Internet: www.environmentaldefense.org
Email: members@environmentaldefense.org
Phone: (212) 505-2100; (800) 684-3322
Fax: (212) 505-2375
Mail: 275 Park Avenue South, New York, NY 10010
for the main office; 1875 Connecticut Ave, NW, Ste. 600,
Washington, DC 20009 for membership and public information

Friends of the Earth

What is the organization's mission?

To defend the environment and work toward a healthy and just world.

How will the organization spend my money?

Donations are used to expose environmental health hazards and injustices in the U.S. and abroad and to urge the government to change things for the better.

Break it down!

Sixty-nine cents of every dollar go to initiatives. Twenty cents go to managing the organization and eleven cents to fund-raising.

Anything else I should know?

Friends of the Earth operates in over 70 countries.

How can I donate or get more information on this charity?

Internet: www.foe.org
Email: foe@foe.org
Phone: (877) 843-8687
Fax: (202) 783-0444
Mail: 1717 Massachusetts Avenue, NW,
Suite 600, Washington, DC 20036

Greenpeace

What is the organization's mission?

To use peaceful, direct action and creative ways of communicating to expose the world's environmental problems; to promote solutions that allow for a green and peaceful future with a healthy environment.

How will the organization spend my money?

Donations are used towards campaigns that help protect our oceans, forests, land, air and water; reduce global warming and toxins in the environment; and fight against nuclear development and genetic engineering in food crops.

Break it down!

Seventy-nine cents of every dollar donated to Greenpeace go directly to programs. Sixteen cents go to fund-raising and the remaining five cents go towards management.

Anything else I should know?

Greenpeace was formed when the United States said it was going to test nuclear weapons on Amchitka Island in 1971. A few people decided to fight against it, so they journeyed across the cold Pacific Ocean to protest the harmful testing. They called themselves "Greenpeace."

How can I donate or get more information on this charity?

Internet: www.greenpeace.org
Email: info@wdp.greenpeace.org
Phone: (202) 462-1177; (800) 326-0959
Fax: (202) 462-4507
Mail: 702 H Street, NW, Ste. 300, Washington, DC 20001

Inform, Inc.

What is the organization's mission?

To look at how businesses affect the environment and human
health and find ways in which businesses can experience
economic growth without harming the environment.

How will the organization spend my money?

Inform, Inc. conducts and publishes research in three key areas:
waste prevention and reduction, sustainable transportation and
alternative fuels, and the effects of toxic chemicals on human
health.

Break it down!

About 76 cents of every dollar go to the program services. Two
cents go to fund-raising and 22 cents go to management.

Anything else I should know?

Inform, Inc. has published over 100 reports on how to avoid
unsafe uses of toxic chemicals, protect land and water resources,
conserve energy, and safeguard public health.

How can I donate or get more information on this charity?

Internet: www.informinc.org
Email: ramsey@informinc.org
Phone: (212) 361-2400
Fax: (212) 361-2412
Mail: 120 Wall Street, New York, NY 10005-4001

Izaak Walton League of America

What is the organization's mission?

To protect the water, soil, forest, and natural resources of America and other countries and to educate the public about how to use and enjoy them.

How will the organization spend my money?

The league educates citizens and lawmakers about wildlife habitat, clean air and water, renewable energy, sustainable agriculture, responsible outdoor behavior, sustainable forestry, and more. They provide citizens with the knowledge and the tools to become active conservationists.

Break it down!

Seventy-nine cents of every dollar are spent on conservation and education programs. Seven cents go to fund-raising and 14 cents go to administrative services

Anything else I should know?

Izaak Walton was an English fisherman in the 1600s. He wrote the literary classic *The Compleat Angler*. He became a symbol in 1922 for 54 men who wanted to improve the condition of America's polluted fishing streams.

How can I donate or get more information on this charity?

Internet: www.iwla.org
Email: general@iwla.org
Phone: (800) 453-5463
Fax: (301) 548-0146
Mail: 707 Conservation Lane, Gaithersburg, MD 20878

National Audubon Society

What is the organization's mission?

To conserve and restore ecosystems, with special attention to birds, other wildlife, and their habitats for the benefit of the Earth's biodiversity and of mankind.

How will the organization spend my money?

Its national network of community-based nature centers and chapters, scientific and educational programs, and advocacy on behalf of areas sustaining important bird populations engage millions of people of all ages and backgrounds in positive conservation experiences.

Break it down!

Seventy-four cents of every dollar go towards program services, five cents go to management expenses, and 21 cents go to fund-raising.

Anything else I should know?

The society is named after the world-famous bird artist and naturalist John James Audubon.

How can I donate or get more information on this charity?

Internet: www.audubon.org
Email: donations@audubon.org
Phone: (212) 979-3000
Fax: (212) 979-3188
Mail: 700 Broadway, New York, NY 10003

National Parks Conservation Association

What is the organization's mission?

To enhance and protect the national park system for people today and for future generations.

How will the organization spend my money?

It assesses how healthy the parks are and how well they're being cared for; it educates decision makers, lawmakers, and the public about how important it is to protect the parks; and it fights for laws that protect the parks.

Break it down!

Seventy-five cents out of every dollar go to programs. Eleven cents go to fund-raising and 14 cents go to administrative costs.

Anything else I should know?

The organization began over 85 years ago and now has over 300,000 members.

How can I donate or get more information on this charity?

Internet: www.npca.org
Email: npca@npca.org
Phone: (800) 628-7275
Fax: (202) 659-0650
Mail: 1300 19th Street, NW, Suite 300, Washington, DC 20036

National Resources Defense Council

What is the organization's mission?
To safeguard the Earth, including the plants, the animals, the people, and the natural systems that make life possible.

How will the organization spend my money?
It will be spent to work for cleaner air, energy, and water; to stop global warming; and to protect endangered natural places through activism and education.

Break it down!
Eighty-one cents out of every dollar go to environmental program work. Twelve cents go to fund-raising and seven cents go to management.

Anything else I should know?
The organization is supported by over one million members.

How can I donate or get more information on this charity?
Internet: www.nrdc.org
Email: nrdcinfo@nrdc.org
Phone: (212) 727-2700
Fax: (212) 727-1773
Mail: 40 West 20th Street, New York, NY 10011

The Nature Conservancy

What is the organization's mission?

To protect the land and water needed in order for Earth's diverse plants, animals, and natural communities to survive.

How will the organization spend my money?

The Nature Conservancy's vision is to conserve portfolios of functional conservation areas within and across ecoregions. By 2015, The Nature Conservancy will work with others to ensure the effective conservation of places that represent at least 10% of every major habitat type on Earth.

Break it down!

Approximately 78 cents of every dollar go to The Nature Conservancy. Twelve cents are used administratively and ten cents are used for fund-raising.

Anything else I should know?

The Nature Conservancy has protected over 5,000 miles of river and 117 million acres of land around the world.

How can I donate or get more information on this charity?

Internet: www.tnc.org
Email: comment@tnc.org
Phone: (800) 628-6860
Fax: none
Mail: 4245 N. Fairfax Drive, Ste. 100, Arlington, VA 22203

The Ocean Conservancy

What is the organization's mission?

To ensure that the world has wild, healthy oceans with diverse natural ecosystems, abundant marine wildlife, and clean water.

How will the organization spend my money?

Donations are used to do research, educate people, and conduct science-based advocacy that will inspire people to speak and act in support of the world's oceans.

Break it down!

Nearly 79 cents of every dollar are used to protect marine wildlife and habitats. About seven cents go to management and 14 cents to fund-raising.

Anything else I should know?

The International Costal Cleanup is a major international volunteer effort for cleaner oceans that spans 90 countries and draws between 300,000 and 500,000 participants worldwide. On the third Saturday in September, volunteers clean up trash from their local beaches, lakes, rivers, and waterways; record what they find; and return the data to The Ocean Conservancy. The data is used to help advocate for cleaner beaches. You can visit www.CoastalCleanup.org for more information.

How can I donate or get more information on this charity?

Internet: www.oceanconservancy.org
Email: info@oceanconservancy.org
Phone: (202) 429-5609; (800) 519-1541
Fax: none
Mail: 2029 K Street, NW, 7th Floor, Washington, DC 20006

Pesticide Action Network (PAN)

What is the organization's mission?

To replace pesticide use with other methods that are healthy for the environment and socially fair.

How will the organization spend my money?

PAN links local and international consumer, labor, health, environment, and agriculture groups into an international citizens' action network. This network challenges the global proliferation of pesticides, defends basic rights to health and environmental quality, and works to ensure the transition to a just and viable society.

Break it down!

Ninety-one cents of every dollar go to the programs, three cents to management, and six cents to fund-raising.

Anything else I should know?

PAN also has networks in Africa, Asia, Europe, and Latin America.

How can I donate or get more information on this charity?

Internet: www.panna.org
Email: panna@panna.org
Phone: (415) 981-1771
Fax: (415) 981-1991
Mail: North America Regional Center, 49 Powell Street, Suite 500, San Francisco, CA 94102

Rails-to-Trails Conservancy

What is the organization's mission?

To create a network of public parks and trails along old train rail lines, as a way of enhancing the health of America's environment, economy, neighborhoods, and people.

How will the organization spend my money?

Donations are used to encourage government policy to let trails happen and to help agencies and volunteer citizens to make it happen.

Break it down!

Seventy-five cents of every dollar go directly to the program services. Thirteen cents go to fund-raising and 12 cents go to management expenses.

Anything else I should know?

RTC has assisted hundreds of communities and rail-trail advocates in building more than 13,500 miles of trails. These trails are ideal for biking, walking, skating, cross-country skiing, horseback riding, and wheelchair use.

How can I donate or get more information on this charity?

Internet: www.railtrails.org
Email: membership@railtrails.org
Phone: (202) 331-9696
Fax: (202) 331-9680
Mail: 1100 17th St, NW, 10th Floor, Washington, DC 20036

Rainforest Action Network

What is the organization's mission?

To campaign for the forests, their inhabitants, and the natural systems that sustain life by transforming the global marketplace through education, grassroots organizing, and non-violent direct action.

How will the organization spend my money?

RAN spends donations by nurturing a grassroots movement capable of convincing huge corporations that environmentally and socially destructive practices are not okay. As a result, Citigroup, Burger King, Bank of America, Boise Cascade, and others have adopted comprehensive environmental and social policies.

Break it down!

About 75 cents of every dollar go to programs. The rest covers fund-raising and management costs.

Anything else I should know?

Rainforests make up just 2% of the Earth's surface, but contain over half the plant and animal species that exist. Tragically, 78 million acres of this precious land—and the plants, animals, and people that live there—are being destroyed every year.

How can I donate or get more information on this charity?

Internet: www.ran.org
Email: rainforest@ran.org
Phone: (415) 398-4404
Fax: (415) 398-2732
Mail: 221 Pine St., Suite 500, San Francisco, CA 94104

Rainforest Alliance

What is the organization's mission?

To protect ecosystems and the people and wildlife that depend on them by transforming land-use practices, business practices, and consumer behavior.

How will the organization spend my money?

Donations are used for education, training, outreach, and partnership building among businesses, governments, and local peoples.

Break it down!

Eighty cents of every dollar go to the programs. Fourteen cents are put toward management and administration, and the other six cents go to fund-raising.

Anything else I should know?

The Rainforest Alliance has an Adopt-a-Rainforest program through which you can support a small conservation group that's trying to save the rainforest in a Central or South American country.

How can I donate or get more information on this charity?

Internet: www.rainforest-alliance.org
Email: info@ra.org
Phone: (212) 677-1900; (888) MY-EARTH
Fax: (212) 677-2187
Mail: 665 Broadway, Suite 500, New York, NY 10012

The Rocky Mountain Institute

What is the organization's mission?

To encourage the efficient use of resources, so the world can be more secure, prosperous, and life sustaining.

How will the organization spend my money?

Donations help the institute research and apply practical ways to help the environment by improving communities, businesses, and even governments. It helps citizens by providing cleaner air, better use of resources, and less strain on our environment.

Break it down!

Seventy-four cents of every dollar go directly to programs. Ten cents go to fund-raising. Sixteen cents go to management.

Anything else I should know?

The institute's web site offers visitors lots of tips on how to reduce the amount of energy they use in their homes and cars.

How can I donate or get more information on this charity?

Internet: www.rmi.org
Email: through web site
Phone: (970) 927-3851
Fax: (970) 927-3420
Mail: 1739 Snowmass Creek Road, Snowmass, CO 81654-9199

Scenic America

What is the organization's mission?

To preserve and enhance the scenic character of America's communities and countryside.

How will the organization spend my money?

Scenic America fights against the placement of billboards along highways and advocates for local, state, and federal laws to preserve and enhance open space and the distinctive character of communities.

Break it down!

Seventy-seven cents of each dollar is put to the programs, while 16 cents go to administration, and seven to fund-raising.

Anything else I should know?

Their motto is "Change is inevitable. Ugliness is not."

How can I donate or get more information on this charity?

Internet: www.scenic.org
Email: scenic@scenic.org
Phone: (202) 638-0550
Fax: (202) 638-3171
Mail: 1634 I Street, NW, Suite 510, Washington, DC 20006

The Sierra Club Foundation

What is the organization's mission?

To preserve and protect the natural environment by getting charitable resources to citizens and grassroots organizations.

How will the organization spend my money?

Working as a funding resource for the environmental community, the foundation offers its services in receiving, administering, and disbursing funds for tax-exempt charitable, scientific, literary, and educational purposes both to the Sierra Club and to other environmental organizations and projects.

Break it down!

Ninety cents of every dollar go to the programs. Three cents go towards running the organization and seven cents go to fund-raising.

Anything else I should know?

While the foundation is autonomous and is governed by its own Board of Trustees, it works closely with the Sierra Club in pursuing its program and goals.

How can I donate or get more information on this charity?

Internet: www.tscf.org
Email: sierraclub.foundation@sierraclub.org
Phone: (415) 995-1780
Fax: none
Mail: 85 Second Street, Suite 750, San Francisco, CA 94105

Student Conservation Association (SCA)

What is the organization's mission?

To educate students to become conservation leaders through hands-on service and environmental programs in America's national parks, forests, cultural treasures, and urban green spaces.

How will the organization spend my money?

The largest and oldest group of its type in America, SCA organizes interns and volunteers to provide over 1.5 million hours of service to the environment each year at nearly 400 different locations around the nation.

Break it down!

Eighty-six cents of every dollar go to the programs, while eight cents go to management, and six cents go to fund-raising.

Anything else I should know?

SCA has been recognized by the White House for its achievements in conservation.

How can I donate or get more information on this charity?

Internet: www.thesca.org
Email: through web site
Phone: (603) 543-1700
Fax: (603) 543-1828
Mail: P.O. Box 550, Charlestown, NH 03603

The Surfrider Foundation

What is the organization's mission?

To protect and preserve the world's oceans, waves, and beaches through conservation, activism, research, and education.

How will the organization spend my money?

Donations are used to support volunteer programs such as water-quality monitoring, beach cleanups, and other mission-related initiatives and educational activities.

Break it down!

Approximately 86 cents of every dollar go directly to programs.

Seven cents go to administration and seven cents go to fund-raising.

Anything else I should know?

The Surfrider Foundation has over 50,000 members and 63 chapters across the country.

How can I donate or get more information on this charity?

Internet: www.surfrider.org
Email: info@surfrider.org
Phone: (800) 743-SURF
Fax: (949) 492-8170
Mail: P.O. Box 6010, San Clemente, CA 92674-6010

Trust for Public Land

What is the organization's mission?

To better the lives of Americans and their communities by conserving land for recreation.

How will the organization spend my money?

It works with landowners, government agencies, and community groups to preserve open space from development and create more beautiful, natural areas.

Break it down!

Eighty-eight cents of every dollar go to the programs, ten cents go to overhead, and two cents go to fund-raising.

Anything else I should know?

Since 1972, the trust has protected nearly two million acres of open space in the United States.

How can I donate or get more information on this charity?

Internet: www.tpl.org
Email: info@tpl.org
Phone: (415) 495-4014
Fax: (415) 495-4103
Mail: 116 New Montgomery Street, 4th Floor,
San Francisco, CA 94105

The Wilderness Society

What is the organization's mission?

To give future generations an unspoiled legacy of wild places, with all of their precious "diversity, clean air and water, towering forests, rushing rivers, and sage-sweet, silent deserts."

How will the organization spend my money?

They use scientific knowledge and analysis, and boldly advocate on behalf of wilderness environments.

Break it down!

About 74 cents of every dollar go to program services. Four cents go to administration and 22 cents go to fund-raising.

Anything else I should know?

The Wilderness Society helped pass the Wilderness Act of 1964, which set aside nine million acres of land as "wilderness."

How can I donate or get more information on this charity?

Internet: www.wilderness.org
Email: member@tws.org
Phone: (800) THE-WILD
Fax: none
Mail: 1615 M Street, NW, Washington, DC 20036

NOTES

NOTES